W9-BJE-097

God Makes Me Laugh

A New Approach to Luke

by

Joseph A. Grassi

Michael Glazier
Wilmington, Delaware

About the Author

Joseph A. Grassi is a professor in the Department of Religious Studies at Santa Clara University. He studied Theology and Scripture at Rome, where he earned his S.S.L. degree at the Pontifical Biblical Institute. His principal area of research is the New Testament and Christian Origins. Among his previous books are *The Secret of Paul the Apostle* and *Broken Bread and Broken Bodies: The Lord's Supper and World Hunger.* He has contributed articles to the *Jerome Biblical Commentary* (Ephesians, Colossians) and has written for the *Catholic Biblical Quarterly, Bible Today, New Testament Studies,* and *Novum Testamentum.*

First published in 1986 by Michael Glazier, Inc.
1935 W. Fourth Street, Wilmington, DE 19805

©1986 by Michael Glazier, Inc.

Library of Congress Catalog Card Number: 85-45552
International Standard Book Numbers:
  Good News Studies: 0-89453-290-1
  God Makes Me Laugh: 0-89453-540-4

Typography by Debbie L. Farmer
Printed in the United States of America.

GOOD NEWS STUDIES

Consulting Editor: Robert J. Karris, O.F.M.

1. Call to Discipleship: A Literary Study of Mark's Gospel
   by Augustine Stock, O.S.B.

2. Becoming Human Together
   The Pastoral Anthropology of St. Paul
   by Jerome Murphy-O'Connor, O.P.

3. Light of All Nations
   Studies on the Church in New Testament Research
   by Daniel Harrington, S.J.

4. Palestinian Judaism and the New Testament
   by Martin McNamara, M.S.C.

5. The Apocalypse: The Perennial Revelation of Jesus Christ
   by Eugenio Corsini
   Translated and Edited by Francis Moloney, S.D.B.

6. St. Paul's Corinth: Texts & Archaeology
   by Jerome Murphy-O'Connor, O.P.

7. A New Look at Preaching
   Walter J. Burghardt/Raymond E. Brown, et. al.

8. A Galilean Rabbi and His Bible
   Jesus' Use of the Interpreted Scripture of His Time
   by Bruce D. Chilton

9. The Unity of Luke's Theology: An Analysis of Luke-Acts
   by Robert F. O'Toole, S.J.

10. Experiencing the Good News: New Testament as Communication
    by James M. Reese, O.S.F.S.

11. Leadership in Paul
    by Helen Doohan

12. Gospel Love: A Narrative Theology
    by John Navone, S.J.

13. Christ is Community: The Christologies of the New Testament
    by Jerome H. Neyrey, S.J.

14. The Sermon on the Mount: Proclamation and Exhortation
    by Jan Lambrecht, SJ

15. People of the Resurrection
    by Lionel Swain

16. The Early Christians: Their World Mission & Self-Discovery
    by Ben Meyer

Other Titles in Preparation.

Contents

Introduction 7

1. Divine and Human Laughter:
   The Roots of Cosmic Eschatology 14
2. Comedy Scene at the River Jordan 22
3. The Stern Baptist and the Nazarene Clown 30
4. Miracles and Comic Reversals 38
5. Feasts of Fools 48
6. Crazy Discipleship:
   The Sermon on the Plain 57
7. Is a Woman's Place at Home? 65
8. The Sign of Jonah the Comic Prophet 73
9. Paradoxical Parables 83
10. Spectacular Parties for the Hungry 92
11. The Kingdom is Child's Play 98
12. Humor in Prayer or Answer Before You Ask 106
13. Throw Your Money Away 114
14. Foolish Forgiveness 123
15. A Donkey Teaches the Way to
    Peace Through Non-Violence 132
16. The End Is the Beginning 141

Bibliography 147
Scripture Index 149

Introduction

God has made me laugh. These title words are taken from the bible itself. Sarah, Abraham's wife, was so astonished when she gave birth to a child in her old age that the only reaction she had was laughter. She said, "God has made me laugh, and all who hear about it will laugh with me" (Genesis 21:6). These words sum up a biblical theme that God's ways are so mysterious and unusual that they provoke laughter from human beings. Biblical belief concerns the impossible from a human standpoint—something laughable and ridiculous. In fact, if it can't be laughed about, it really can't be believed at all, since it would fall within the realm of human abilities.

This biblical theme is often forgotten in practice because the bible is such a serious and sacred book that laughter seems out of place. Especially for Christians, the gospels are *serious* matters—and Christians tend to be serious people. Surely the gospel message concerns eternal salvation and is no joking matter. In addition, the pages of the gospel seem to contain no descriptions of a laughing and smiling Jesus. He appears totally engaged about the message of the kingdom, about matters of life and death. His words and actions lead to a bitter cross, not a stage show. Those who follow his example must expect suffering and embrace the way of the cross.

Yet the very Scriptures themselves contain comic literature. Jesus would be following a long biblical tradition if he recognized this and built upon it. The books of Ruth, Jonah and Qoheleth are definitely comic literature. The book of Ruth is delightful piece of post-exilic literature reacting to the very narrow views of Jewish leaders such as Nehemiah and Ezra. These leaders had even demanded that Jews who had not gone into exile should break up their marriages with non-Jews and abandon wives and children who were not of pure Jewish blood (Ezr. 9:10; Neh. 13:1-3, 23-28). This was a strict interpretation and extension of Deuteronomy 23:4, which read, "No Ammonite or Moabite may be admitted into the community of the Lord, nor any descendent of theirs to the tenth generation." Instead the book of Ruth presents Ruth, a Moabite, as even the ancestor of David the king, which is about as far as a person could go in humorous contrast. Not only that, she is presented as a model of virtue far surpassing that of any Jewish woman.

The story of Jonah deals with the same universal theme in the most comic possible manner. It is unheard of that God would send a Hebrew prophet to the Jew's worst enemies, the people of Babylon. Jonah is so amazed and shocked by this order that he takes a ship to Tarshish (Spain and the end of the world in these days) to escape this charge. The story of the fish swallowing him and vomiting him up on land to force him into this mission all adds to the humorous atmosphere of the story. The book of Qoheleth pokes fun at the deadly seriousness of many wisdom teachers and their tradition (Eccl. 2:12-17).

But what about the New Testament? Are these not much more serious documents? They certainly are, but this does not keep them from often conveying what I call a comic eschatology. Some definition of terms is needed. By "eschatology," I mean a view or knowledge about the last things. These "last things" are the fulfilment of the divine plan to intervene on earth and establish a new age, where God would reign as king. Jesus' message and life was about this future kingdom which he felt was about to begin through his own words and actions. As such, it could be the fulfilment of God's great plan as announced in the Holy Scriptures. By "comic" I mean that this eschatology is accomplished in such a strikingly different way from ordinary human expectations that it becomes a matter for surprise, wonder and laughter, when people realize the extreme paradox.

Why select Luke-Acts? Would it not be better to go through a careful comparison of documents and sources to recover the earthly historical Jesus, instead of using a writer who is obviously secondary, by his own words? (Luke 1:1-2) In response, it should be said that there are signs that "the quest for the historical Jesus" has come to a near impasse despite the work of great scholars of the past 30 or 40 years such as Bultmann, Jeremias, Bornhamm, Käsemann, Robinson, Perrin and many others. Perhaps the "fault" lies in the sources themselves which never intended to write ancient history or documentaries for modern scholars. The gospel writers wanted to convey "good news" to their own audience. They had in mind to conserve not primarily the exact wording to Jesus' statements, or a precise description of what he did, but what he, the living one, meant to say here and now for living people.

Let me give an illustration from a comedian of our own century, Will Rogers who died in an airplane crash in the mid-thirties. In his case we have little difficulty with the "Historical Will Rogers." Phonograph recording at his time enables us to have an exact rendition of what he actually said, even the reactions of his audience. The source of his jokes was the daily newspaper. He often said, "All I know is what I read in the newspapers." From the newspapers he would simply point out the ridiculous contrasts between pretensions, ideals, even religion, and what people, including officials, congress and the president say and do. He rarely repeated a joke, considering them stale by the next day. An atmosphere of newness or surprise was considered essential. In fact, much of his material today makes rather dull reading. However, I recently attended a rendition of Will Rogers made by James Whitmore. He skilfully imitated Will Rogers' speech, gestures and tricks, using the exact words from the recordings. However, he selected those sayings which today bring out the same paradox in a new situation. The audience reacted with enthusiastic laughter. Will Rogers had come to life and was speaking to them. In other words it is the element of skilful paradox that made Will Rogers what he was, and makes him meaningful today *if the paradox is recovered for our own time.*

Something like this was true for the evangelists. Jesus' words, proverbs, and actions were a paradox for their own time. A paradox is a special way of insight. It enables us to see things *as they are* instead of according to the models or expectations of most people. When we are able to see the contrast between the two, and actually accept it—especially through laughter and humor—we become open to change. To merely recover the actual words and settings of Jesus' instruction as an exercise of research was not the gospel writers' intention. It would have been boring for themselves and for their audience. Some significant recent biblical research[1] points out that the writers did, however, wish to recover the paradox of the living Jesus for their own audience; this was for them the real historical Jesus.

This leads us back to the question as to why we selected Luke. Actually, we could have selected any other gospel. Each of them wrote because they found ways to preserve the paradox of Jesus for their own time and audience. Each one of them preserves elements of the comic eschatology we are concerned with. However, Luke has read previous writers and seems to find something lacking. He is concerned, as he

---

[1]For example, Werner Kelber in the concluding lines of his book, *The Oral and Written Gospels* writes, "Insofar as the parable is one of Jesus' primary modes of speech, one can say that it furnishes linguistic and theological connection between the speaker in parables and the written gospel. Both gospel and oral parables transcend their respective narratives by pointing to the kingdom of God." Dominic Crossan in a special way has pointed to the uniqueness of Jesus' parables in contrast to earlier Jewish forms. Continuity between the Jesus of history and the Christ of faith is established when the originality of the parable and its paradox becomes again the experience of the gospel audience. He writes, "Continuity can bo found however, where the parabler becomes the Parable, where Jesus who spoke in paradoxes becomes acknowledged as the Paradox of God." D. Crossan, *Raids on the Articulate* p. 177.

mentions in his first verse, "about the things accomplished among us." In other words, about the unfolding of the divine plan he has observed in his own experience of Jesus and in the early church. Modern scholarship has increasingly noted the essential unity of Luke's Gospel and his Acts of the Apostles in their attempt to unfold the fulfilment of the divine plan, first in Jesus' life in the first volume and then in the church's life in the second volume.

Among modern scholars, Hans Conzelmann[2] has drawn attention to the continuity between the period of Israel, the period of Jesus, and the period of the church in both volumes. Eugene LaVerdiere has followed this basic outline in his commentary on Luke in the New Testament Message Series. He writes:

> All three eras spell out the history of God's Word, how it came to John as it had come to Israel before him, was manifested by Jesus and continued to spread and develop through the life and mission of the Church. Continuity also came through the Holy Spirit, whose creative energy enables salvation history to transcend its inherent discontinuities and enable the Word to bridge the chasms which divided the eras.[3]

While Luke certainly had other purposes in mind as he wrote, this dominant theme of the realization of God's plan places other motives in a secondary and subservient role. Robert O'Toole[4] has examined all these latter claims and has not found them sufficient to explain Luke's motivation. O'Toole culminated his studies in his book on the *Unity of Luke's Theology.*[5] In it he expresses his central thesis that the God who brought salvation to his people in the Old

---

[2] *Theology of St. Luke,* pp. 16-17

[3] *Luke*, p. xxxi

[4] O'Toole, R., "Why Did Luke Write Acts (Lk-Acts?") *Biblical Theology Bulletin* 7 (1977) 66-72.

[5] cf. bibliography

Testament continued his plan by doing so through Jesus in his earthly life, and then through Jesus in his church. The continuity of God's plan thus remains primary.

However, this planned fulfilment is by no means like a dull printout of a computerized divine program. As we go through his gospel, we will find that our author has many new insights about how this divine plan has been accomplished in such a surprising and unusual manner that it results in laughter and astonishment on the part of those who experience it. Robert Karris[6] has given special attention to this aspect in Luke-Acts. He notes the following: "We are not only surprised by the unexpected, but unless we expect the unexpected we will not find truth." For this reason we have selected Luke as our author in order to have a better picture of comic eschatology, where Jesus is often seen as a "jokester" presenting new and humourous contrasts between God's views of the kingdom and the ordinary expectations and models of many people, especially religious leaders. Sarah said, "God has made me laugh, *so that those who hear about it may laugh with me.*" Her words sum up a purpose of this book: if the reader at least smiles or laughs occasionally, it will be a sign that the paradoxical presence of Jesus has been recovered and assimilated.

Another reason for our selection of Luke is found in his strong sense of continuity between the Jesus in the gospel, the Jesus in the early church, and the Jesus experienced by himself and the communities he addresses. R. O'Toole[7] has placed special emphasis on this theme of continuity. The very same Jesus who walked on earth, taught his disciples, healed and touched the people who came to him was the one present to the early church and to Luke's communities. This Jesus as risen Lord was present in eucharistic gatherings (24:31,35), in the preaching of witnesses (Acts 3:22-23; 18:5-11; 26:23), through visions (Acts 7:55-56; 9:1-19), signs and wonders (Acts 4:29-30), through the Holy Spirit (Luke 24:49; Acts 1:2,8; 2:33,38,39; 16:6-7), and through his pow-

[6] *What Are They Saying About Luke and Acts*, p. 55
[7] This is a principal theme in his book, *The Unity of Luke's Theology*.

erful name (Acts 2:21,38; 3:6,16; 4:12; 10:43; 16:18). What Luke presents in his gospel is not time limited but a continual divine and comic paradox that readers and listeners can enter into again and again. This book is meant to facilitate the process for the modern reader.

Finally, it is the narrative or story element in Luke that makes his gospel transcend time. While other gospels contain this, Luke goes far beyond them in this unique teaching approach. John Navone[8] highlights this Lukan orientation in his book describing the Jesus story as our own story in Christ. Luke wants his readers to enter into the Jesus story and make it their own. One of Luke's special ways of doing this is by way of special attention to the divine paradoxes so skilfully drawn out in his gospel. When the reader finds that the paradox is his or own as well, then a unique learning situation begins. A first reaction may be somewhat painful, but as the lesson is learned, the joy and surprise of the divine paradox becomes the occasion of new, enthusiastic energy for dynamic Christian living.

[8]In *The Jesus Story: Our Life as Story in Christ,* and also in *Gospel Love: A Narrative Theology,* (Wilmington: Michael Glazier, Inc. 1985).

1

Divine and Human Laughter –

The Roots of Cosmic Eschatology

When people plan, trusting only in human power, God laughs; when God plans, working through human weakness, people laugh, In this paradox is found the roots of cosmic eschatology. "Eschatology" means literally a knowledge or science of the last times. These last times are the great expected future age when the Creator would make his complete and final intervention in the world to restore his human family in justice and peace. If this is truly to be God's work, following the Scripture pattern it must be *comic*; it must be a complete surprise; it must make people laugh. Peter Berger[9] suggests that "there is one fundamental discrepancy from which all other comic discrepancies are derived—the discrepancy between man and universe."

In the very first verse of his two volume work, the Gospel and the Acts of the Apostles, Luke tells us that many have undertaken to write about literally the *things fulfilled among us.* This is a technical term for the divine plan, as

[9]*A Rumor of Angels*, p. 70

found in the Scriptures. In verse three, the author tells us that he also would like to do the same. Why would he go to this trouble, if, as he writes in verse two, many have already written about this? Here we cannot investigate all the motives of the evangelist. However, we wish to point out an important theme that begins to appear in first two chapters, the story of the birth and childhood of Jesus.

This theme is that the fulfilment of Scriptures has taken place in a surprising and unexpected manner. This has resulted in a comic eschatology making people laugh when they become aware of the unusual way that God has acted. Luke reveals this intention by the way he describes the events with special reference to the paradoxical and laughable way that God has worked in the decisive formative events in human history. This we will try to outline in the following pages.

We started with the paradoxical expression, "When people plan trusting only in human power, God laughs." This is a scriptural truism based on Psalm 2, where the rulers of the earth plot together to revolt against God and his anointed. In response, the psalmist writes, "From his throne in heaven, the Lord laughs; he derides their feeble plans" (2:2-4). Luke was certainly familiar with these words; he even quotes the first two verses in Acts 4:25-26, applying them to the feeble efforts of Jewish leaders to stop Peter and John from preaching about Jesus.

The second opening paradox was, "When God plans, working through human weakness, people laugh." Luke found this theme in the beginnings of Jewish history, the birth of a son to Abraham and Sarah in their extreme old age. We shall point out later his actual references to that story. In the Old Testament, the whole divine plan to renew creation begins with the call of Abraham. He is told that he and his offspring will be a source of blessing for the whole world: "By you all the families of the earth shall bless themselves" (Gen. 12:3). Even from the start, the whole matter has an impossible tone about it. Abraham was already 75 years old (12:4) and his wife was 9 years younger. The elderly couple did not at first understand the words as referring to a natural offspring. Sarah pressed Abraham to take a second wife, Hagar an Egyptian slave girl, so they could adopt a child as their own (Gen. 16:1). As a result, Ishmael was born, whom they supposed to be their heir.

However, God appeared to Abraham and said that Sarah his wife would actually bear a son and become a mother of nations. This was simply too much for old Abraham. He bowed to the ground and could not refrain from laughing. He said to himself, "Shall a child be born to a man who is hundred years old? Shall Sarah, who is ninety years old, bear a child?" (Gen, 17:13-18) Sarah also had a hearty laugh when she overheard one of three mysterious strangers (angels in disguise?) predict that she would have a child in the coming year. Sarah laughed and said to herself, "After I have grown old, and my husband is old, shall I have pleasure?" (18:12). The writer wishes to make a key point of this laughter, for he notes that the Lord said to Abraham, "Why did Sarah laugh and say, 'Shall I indeed bear a child now that I am old?'" Sarah became afraid and denied it saying, "I didn't laugh." But God replied, "Yes you did, you laughed" (18:13-15).

Finally the promised child was born and Sarah exclaimed. "God has made me laugh; all those who hear of it will laugh with me." She said, "Who would have told Abraham that Sarah would nurse children? Yet I have borne him a child in his old age" (Gen. 21:6-7). So the child was called Isaac, which means "laughter." Faith in God concerns the humanly impossible; it is literally *ridiculous* in its root meaning from the Latin *ridere*, to laugh. It is this ridiculous element that Luke will emphasize in his first two chapters to set the framework for a comic eschatology in the rest of his gospel.

The scene of the gospel opens with Zechariah the holy priest officiating at the altar of incense in the sacred chamber in front of the Holy of Holies. Luke intends to present him as representative of those who are slow to welcome the great divine surprise of the eschatological era. In contrast, Mary will be presented as the model for the believer willing to accept the "upside-down" and comic way (according to human standards) that God chooses to act in the final age.

Like Abraham and Sarah, Zechariah and Elizabeth are old and advanced in years. The greatest blessing of life, the birth of a child had been denied them. Yet they had "everything going" for them. He was a priest. They were both perfect observers of the justice of the law. Not to have a child exposed them to human ridicule, for this condition was commonly considered to be a sign of the loss of God's favor, perhaps due to secret sins. Since there were so many priests, Zechariah took his turn in priestly service with other members of his group or class. To offer incense before the Holy of Holies was an extraordinary and rare duty, so it was decided by lot. It could be considered a once-in-a-lifetime privilege. As he prayed and offered incense, the rest of the people, not permitted to enter the holy Temple itself, remained outside praying. No doubt they would be praying for the greatest blessing of all, the coming of God's great Messianic age.

Meanwhile, the angel Gabriel appeared to Zechariah and announced, similar to Abraham, the birth of a child in the couple's old age. This in itself was a tremendous shock to a man who had believed that this time of hope was long past. But something more was added that made the child's birth even more extraordinary: he was to be the long awaited messenger to announce the opening of the final new age—in other words the most important person in countless thousands of years of world history. Zechariah knew this because the angel Gabriel described the boy using the last words of the last written prophet of the Old Testament, Malachi. God announced through him that he would send the prophet Elijah before the great day of the Lord to turn the hearts of children to their parents and parents to their children (Mal. 3:24). Zechariah hesitated; it was simply too much for him—a child in old age, the great forerunner of the new age, and Elijah returned to earth. He asked for some visible sign or miracle: "How shall I know this?" he said, "I am an old man and my wife is advanced in years" (1:8). Zechariah must have imagined the ridicule and laughter to which he would expose himself and his wife if he ever told people that this was to happen and then it failed to do so. In this way, he is similar to Abraham. The angel promised no sign except the one Zechariah had imposed on himself. He had chosen to be psychologically dumbfounded, unwilling to speak a word of consent and belief. Now he will be physically dumb, unable to speak until the events come to pass.

Zechariah was so stubborn in his unbelief that it took a shock to shake him out of it. At the child's circumcision, the family was all minded to name him after his father. At this point, Elizabeth, the mother, mindful of the angel's words stood up and took a stand, "No," she said, "John is to be his name" (1:59-66). This was not enough to convince the family. Finally they gave a writing tablet to Zechariah, who confirmed his wife's choice. This was the priest's public affirmation and trust in the angel Gabriel's command that the child was to be called John (1:13). At this point, Luke notes that Zechariah's tongue was loosed and he began to prophesy, announcing to all that the promises made to Abraham were being fulfilled and that the boy was to be the great prophet of the most high promised by the prophet Malachi (1:13).

On the complete opposite side of the spectrum, Luke presents Mary the mother of Jesus as the model[10] for the believer willing to accept God's laughter and embrace the divine paradox of his action through the most impossible and weakest human instruments. Mary stands in deliberate contrast to Zechariah, the respected priest. She is a simple woman from a little town unnamed in the O.T. To become a mother in old age is a remarkable miracle; to become a mother for a virgin is a human absurdity. Luke heightens the contrast by describing Mary in terms similar to Hannah, the mother of Samuel in the O.T. (1 Sam. chaps. 1 and 2). Hannah was a second wife of Elhanah, but for many years had no child. Her rival Peninnah had many sons and daughters, and thus received the preponderance of shares at the

---

[10]This aspect of Mary is brought out in *Mary in the New Testament* esp. p. 137.

temple sacrificial banquets each year. She continually ridic-
uled Hannah who had no children, and thus received only
one portion. In desperation, Hannah went to the Temple to
pray, vowing to give her child in service to the Temple, if
God would grant her one. Because her lips moved in silent
prayer, Eli, the Temple priest even thought she was drunk
and advised her to rid herself of wine. When the priest
learned of her vow, he dismissed her with a blessing. Trusting in this, Hannah returned home where she conceived a
son and later fulfilled her vow.

The resemblances to Hannah are brought out in Luke's
portrait of Mary. Her new name is the "grace-filled one,"
from the Greek root *charis*, meaning grace or favor. This in
turn is a translation of *hen,* from which the name of Hannah
is derived; the English form of this is Anne. In addition, the
words of Mary's Magnificat have a remarkable similarity to
Hannah's thanksgiving song after presenting her child to the
Lord (1 Sam. 2:1-10; Luke 1:46-55).

Luke however, parallels Mary even more to Abraham
and Sarah. The angel assures her with the same words,
"Nothing shall be impossible with God" (1:37; Gen. 18:14).
Mary's word of assent, "Be it done to me according to your
word," are similar to those used by the author of Genesis to
describe God's action in Sarah: "The Lord did to Sarah
according to his word." (Gen. 21:1) Also, as Laurentin[11] has
pointed out, the angel addresses Mary in the same way as
Abraham, who *found grace before God* (Gen. 18:3; Luke
1:30). Both will be the cause of a universal blessing (Gen.
12:3; Luke 1:48). Another dramatic Lukan description of
Mary is in terms of the Temple or holy Ark of the Covenant.
To describe the supreme contrast brought about in Mary
through God's action, the angel says to her, "The Holy
Spirit will come over you and the power of the Most Highj
will overshadow you" (1:35). The word "overshadow" is the
same Greek word used to describe the overshadowing cloud
that filled the Temple after Moses had finished its construc-

---

[11]*Structure et Théologie de Luc I-II*, p. 85. The author also presents details of
the comparison between Luke 1:39-44 and 2 Sam. 6:2-11 where David brings the
Ark to Jerusalem and Mary visits Elizabeth. (pp. 71-73)

tion (Ex. 40:34-35). This would point to a possible Lukan picture of Mary as a Temple of God in human flesh because of the working of the Spirit.

This becomes more than a hint when Luke describes Mary's visit to her cousin Elizabeth. Here there are remarkable parallels[12] to the O.T. legend of David's bringing of the Holy Ark of God to Jerusalem in 2 Sam 6. In the O.T. story David takes 30,000 troops to accompany the Ark of God from the priest Abinadab's house located on a hill in Judea (2 Sam. 6:3). In parallel, Mary visits the home of Elizabeth in the hill country of Judea (Luke 1:39). When a priest named Uzzah was struck down for touching the Ark, David was overcome by fear and exclaimed, "How can the Ark of the Lord come to me?" (6:9) David then had the Ark stay in the house of Obed-edom three months (6:11). In Luke's parallel account, Elizabeth says (literally) to Mary, "How can the Mother of my Lord come to me," and Mary stays three months at Elizabeth's house (1:43). Finally the O.T. story emphasizes David's joyful dancing before the Ark (6:4,14,21) He did this despite the fact that his wife Michael made fun of him for doing so. He replied to her. "It is for the Lord I dance, not for them (the people)" (2 Sam 6:21). Luke specifically mentions that when Elizabeth heard Mary's greeting, the child in her womb leaped (Greek word for dance) for joy.

Altogether, Luke presents a rather impressive picture of Mary as a new Ark of God because of the overshadowing presence of the Spirit of God. Perhaps the evangelist has in mind the biblical story of the hiding of the Ark of God by Jeremiah (2 Macc. 2:5) when the Babylonians sacked Jerusalem. The Ark was never found again, giving rise to all kinds of legends about it, including the phantasy presented by a modern movie, "Raiders of the Lost Ark." Luke may be telling us that the New Age opens with a finding of the Ark

[12]The similarities in the two passages are certainly there. Many authors have found them to be sufficient to say that Luke intended to teach that Mary was like the O.T. Ark of the Covenant as she bore within her the divine child. However, R.E. Brown in *The Birth of the Messiah* (p. 344) and others do not find this thesis sufficiently convincing.

in Mary as the Holy Spirit comes upon her to make her a new Temple of God and model for the believer at any time who can have the same experience. This theme of the model believer may be conveyed by Elizabeth's words to Mary, "Blessed is she who has believed that the promises made her by the Lord would be fulfilled." (1:45) This is a link to the reader of the gospel who is invited to find new assurance about the certainty of his/her faith which concerns "the things fulfilled among us" (1:1).

The theme of divine laughter and paradox may also be echoed by the solemn opening of chapter two: "Now a decree went forth from Caesar Augustus that a census of the whole world was to be taken." The motive, of course, was taxation and complete control. Yet God laughs at human plans. It is the very action of the Roman emperor that makes possible the fulfilment of the scriptures by having Mary give birth to her child at Bethlehem, where she and her husband had to come for registration. The Roman emperor thus prepares the way for the birth of the very king who can take his place as ruler of the world.

To sum up: Luke finds his source for a comic eschatology in the O.T. Scriptures. There, God's plans working through weak human beings seem so surprising and impossible to achieve that they cause people to laugh in astonishment. We see this especially in the birth of Isaac, the child of laughter. Luke appears to take this theme and apply it, by way of contrast to Zechariah and Mary. Mary becomes the model of the true believer who is open to God's mysterious and astonishing ways in his use of weak human instruments to accomplish his purposes. Humans can only laugh at the story of a virginal conception and the picture of a new Temple and Ark of the Covenant in human flesh. God's ways, however, are comic and upside down according to human standards.

2

The Comedy Scene at the River Jordan

Great expectations for the future were in the heart of every sincere Jew at the time of Jesus, although the situation of the nation was outwardly desperate. The country was occupied by foreign Roman troops who completely ignored the Hebrew God. The Jews were governed in Judea by Roman Procurators whose principal concern was to amass a sizeable "retirement fund" so they could live their older years in comfort and luxury in the Roman capital. Herod, half-Jewish and a greedy Roman puppet king, ruled in Galilee to the north of Judea. The excessive taxation imposed by these rulers drained the life of the Jewish people. This situation was aggravated in Judea by the accumulation of farm property in the hands of rich landowners, especially members of the upper class priestly families who enjoyed Rome's favor. In Galilee, beginning with Herod the Great (37-4 BC) and continuing with his son Herod Antipas, the rapacious family of Herod acquired so much property, that at least a half of the population[13] worked for absentee

---

[13]R.J. Cassidy, *Jesus, Politics and Society. A Study of Luke's Gospel.* (Maryknoll, N.Y.: Orbis, 1978) Appendix II, pp. 99-113 deals with social and economic factors. On the Herods and property, cf. pp. 108-109.

landowners, or were reduced to the position of seasonal day laborers.

However, as the outer situation became more desperate, the inner hopes and expectations of the people became more and more intense. In the past, God had sent Moses to liberate them from oppression and slavery in a much more desperate situation in Egypt. He had brought them back to their own land after their exile in Babylon. He was a God of history who would again intervene in a great "Day of the Lord" that would surpass anything he had done in the past. The whole atmosphere in Israel seethed with this urgent expectation. Many people believed it was imminent and could happen at any moment.

The Scriptures pointed to a chosen messenger of the Lord who would suddenly appear to announce this great day of the Lord and prepare the people. The last words of Malachi, the last writing prophet of the Hebrew Scripture had described this messenger in the following striking terms:

> Behold, I will send you Elijah the prophet before the great and terrible day of the LORD comes. And he will turn the hearts of fathers to their children, and the hearts of children to their fathers, lest I come and smite the land with a curse. (4:5-6)

Elijah was a most unusual prophet who had appeared in Israel at a time (9th cent. B.C.) when popular fertility cults had almost smothered the worship of the God of Moses. Elijah was a stern figure clothed in hairy garments and a leather belt (2K. 1:7) who did not hesitate to risk his life to call both king and people to renewal. The unusual manner of his assumption to God through a fiery chariot bringing him to heaven (2K. 2:11) made many people believe he did not really die at all but was being kept at God's side to return to earth before the great day of the Lord.

We can imagine the messianic excitement and fever at Jerusalem when news arrived that a strange Elijah-like figure had appeared by the Jordan River and was announcing that the Kingdom of God was close at hand. Large crowds from Jerusalem and surrounding areas as far north as Galilee travelled to the Jordan river near Jericho to witness the strange goings-on and to listen to the fiery preacher of the last times. Among them was a young carpenter named Jesus from faraway Nazareth who had made the long and difficult journey of some 70-80 miles to be at John's side by the Jordan. What Jesus and the crowds saw at the Jordan was the most unusual spectacle ever seen in Israel.

To understand this, some background is needed. Most future expectations featured Israel as a shining light to the rest of the world. For example, the great prophet Isaiah announced a vision of the future of these words:

> It shall come to pass in the latter days
> that the mountain of the house of the Lord
> shall be established as the highest of the
> mountain, and shall be raised above the hills
> and all nations shall flow to it. (2:1-2)

However, the scene at the Jordan river was an entirely new twist and surprising interpretation of the ancient prophecies. John was requiring a baptism with water, a pledge of reform and a confession of sins as a sign of entry into the coming kingdom. What John asked was a shocking surprise. Such a baptism was only required of pagan converts to Judaism, not of the ordinary Israelite where circumcision of each male was a formal seal of the covenant. Proselyte baptism was a most serious matter. A candidate was expected to be "born again" and start a whole new life. As such, every phase of life had to be reevaluated. Every relationship had to be reexamined, whether through blood or marriage. Even a profession or work had to be changed if necessary. Absolute priority had to be given to the requirements of the Jewish Torah (Law or Teaching). Every convert had to begin life anew as if a new-born babe. The past was over, forgotten and forgiven as each person began a new life. Luke describes the Baptist as preaching the joyful good news of "a baptism of repentance for the forgiveness of sins" (3:3).

The implications of all this were quickly grasped by the crowds at the Jordan. Those whose situation had been regarded as hopeless by religious leaders flocked to John at the Jordan, confessing their sins and receiving his baptism as a preparation for the coming New Age. The Baptist did not give them a complex set of regulations to confuse them, but sweeping new directions of life, based on unselfish giving and sharing.

> The multitudes asked him, "What then shall we do?" And he answered them, "He who has two coats, let him share with him who has none; and he who has food, let him do likewise." (3:10)

The Evangelist singles out two groups, tax collectors and soldiers, whose presence shocked every pious Jew, especially teachers of religion. Tax collectors were not just members of a profession but agents of hated foreign oppressors. They frequently bought their offices from the Romans by offering the highest bid for them. Tax collectors took a precentage of the collections as their salary. Since many of them became rich, the ordinary people felt that these agents of Rome were frequently guilty of fraud and cheating. Soldiers were the necessary cohorts of the tax collectors to maintain order and enforce the collection of taxes. Their position of power was a source of temptation to unfairly requisition food, property and other goods from the ordinary people unless they were "paid off." The Baptist's directions to these two groups hit directly at sincere reform of their practices. Many religious teachers would have insisted that they give up their professions, but John did not require this:

> Tax collectors also came to the baptized, and said to him, "Teacher, what shall we do?" And he said to them "Collect no more than is appointed you." Soldiers also asked him, "And we, what shall we do? And he said to them, "Rob no one by violence or by false accusations, and be content with your wages." (3:12-14)

Another surprise at the Jordan was the appearance of women. Rarely leaving their sheltered homes, they were silent participators in the Synagogue and mere observers at the great initiation rite of circumcision. Yet now they took the initiative to come to John at the Jordan. An even greater shock was the recognition of some prostitutes among them. How could they dare come up to the holy Baptist for baptism and a share in the coming New Age? The presence of women is not noted by Luke but receives special attention from Matthew in these words,

> Jesus said to them, "Truly I say to you, the tax collectors and the harlots go into the kingdom of God before you. For John came to you in the way of righteousness, and you did not believe him, but the tax collectors and the harlots believed him; and even when you saw it, you did not afterward repent and believe him." (21:31-32)

However, the greatest surprise of all was the presence of a group of Jerusalem teachers and leaders who were there as observers and critics rather than participators. These were the Scribes and Pharisees. Matthew also notes their presence (3:7). John's gospel has an official delegation of priests and levites from Jerusalem (1:19). The Scribes (from the Latin root "scribere," to write), were men who dedicated their lives to studying and teaching the Torah. They made the final decisions about application of the Law to legal matters and the affairs of everyday life. They were concerned to apply the Torah to every phase of life. Consequently, they had to continually "update" it by making new decisions and applications to changing circumstances. The Scribes were the respected teachers of Israel in education, in the synagogue and in national life. The Sanhedrin, or 70 member ruling body was comprised largely of Scribes.

Within the Scribes was a smaller group called the Pharisees. Briefly, these latter were a party dedicated to observance of the Torah with meticulous perfection in their personal lives. They even took all the priestly laws of the bible and observed them privately, even though not obliged to do so. They met at regular times to support one another and examine the credentials of prospective new members. The Scribes and especially the Pharisees believed that they could almost "force" the coming of the Kingdom of God through perfect observance of the Torah and by teaching others to do so also. At the Jordan River, they stood by as incredulous and judgemental observers. John was announcing the coming New Age and inviting repentance, change and baptism as if for pagan converts starting life anew. Surely the Baptist's words of reform were not meant for people like themselves who had dedicated their lives to keeping every detail of the written biblical law and its oral interpretation made by generations of teachers before them.

On the other hand John's treatment of sinners as the chosen members of the New Age simply appalled them. The coming kingdom was to be composed of perfect observers of the Law, not of sinners, tax collectors, prostitutes and lawless crowds. Surely at least, the Baptist should give them preferential treatment and respect in view of their dedicated lives and position of authority. To walk into the Jordan River confessing their sins would place them on the same level as the man or woman on the street, which would indeed be foolish. Consequently, they stood apart watching and looking down on something obviously not meant for them. John's Baptist meant radical change for everyone, and of course they did not need change or really want it. It was simply too threatening for them.

Jesus in contrast underwent the baptism of John, standing in the Jordan River surrounded by sinners. Jesus was certainly influenced by the Pharisees[14] and almost by second nature had avoided close contact with "sinners." This was a new and exhilarating experience for him, that would henceforth affect his whole life. He heard the joyful shouts and

---

[14]Luke in particular brings out Jesus' closeness to the Pharisees. He has dinner at their homes. (7:36; 11:37; 14:1) The early Christian church had a number of converted Pharisees. (Acts 15:5) In Matthew and Mark, Jesus' disciples pluck and eat grain on the Sabbath. The Pharisees question Jesus about the disciples' action, not the master's. (Mark 2:23-28; Matt. 12:1-8) Jesus defends the Pharisees authority as teachers, but not their example. (Matt. 23:1-3).

prayers of the crowds beside him in the river. They were simply amazed at the grace of God and their undeserved forgiveness through John's baptism. Looking to the distance, Jesus saw the Scribes and Pharisees standing above the banks of the Jordan. Their stance as "detached observers" was quite evident. Their faces were serious and clouded by the intense speculation going on in their minds. Jesus may have recognized among them several friends, colleagues or even former teachers.

The young carpenter at first saw the tragedy of the whole situation. From his own experience as a Pharisee he knew how hard it was for these men to undergo such a radical change in their lives. Yet a deep insight told him that it could not be God's New Age dawning if it came about through human striving and plans. God's work always turned the tables; it was an "upside down" theology of surprise, grace and shock. Looking at it from this perspective, Jesus smiled as he saw the divine comedy in action through the contrast between the two groups. Here was a visible scene of comic eschatology that could only be described by the ancient saying, "the last shall be first and the first last," a proverb Jesus constantly repeated in his life, probably with a secret smile as he recalled the comic contrast at the Jordan.

Luke's gospel records the vivid impression that the Jordan River scene made upon Jesus. On one occasion, Jesus stated that John the Baptist was the greatest human being ever born yet the very least in the new kingdom were greater than he (7:28). The gospel then adds,

> When they heard this all the people and the tax collectors justified God, having been baptized with the baptism of John; but the Pharisees and the Scribes rejected the purpose of God for themselves, not having been baptized by him. (7:29-30)

On another occasion, the chief priests and scribes questioned Jesus about the source of his authority. Jesus replied by asking the question whether the baptism of John was from heaven or from men. The gospel notes that they could not reply to Jesus because if they stated it was from heaven, Jesus would ask why they did not believe him; if they answered "from men" they feared a violent reaction from the people (20:2-8).

When Luke wrote his gospel, more than 50 or 60 years had elapsed since the events he described. The past for him was so important because he saw comic eschatology as very present in his own experience. He knew Pharisees (Acts 15:8), now Christians who adopted the same attitudes. They added restrictions and regulations for Chrisian converts, even requiring circumcision in addition to baptism, thus setting up a new Christian Torah. (Acts 15:5) In effect, they forgot the repentant muddy waters of the Jordan, and set themselves up as censors, spectators and judges on the safe banks above the river. In effect, Luke places a warning for all future teachers. God's eschatology is always comic. Those who become too serious in their own ideals, models and plans, however lofty, miss the fun and even become part of the tragedy.

3

The Stern Baptist and the Nazarène Clown

The word "clown" conjures up a circus image of a painted figure in fool's costume trying to entertain an audience by tricks, mimicry and jokes. Jesus was not a "clown" in this sense; he was not an entertainer or trickster. However his actions and teaching style were such a striking humorous contrast to the serious conventional piety of his time that the word "clown" would best describe the image he gave to many people. In a Chapter entitled "Christ the Harlequin," Harvey Cox[15] has pointed to a modern re-understanding of the clown aspect of Jesus. In regard to the biblical portrait of Jesus he wrote,

> Like the jester, Christ defies custom and scorns crowned heads. Like a wandering troubador, he has no place to lay his head. Like the clown in the circus parade, he satirizes existing authority by riding into town replete with regal pageantry when he has no earthly power. Like a minstrel, he frequents dinners and parties. At the end he is costumed by his enemies in a mocking caricature of royal

---

[15] *Feast of Fools*, p. 169

paraphernalia. He is crucified amidst snickers and taunts
with a sign over his head that lampoons his laughable
claim. (p. 169)

There are some hints in Luke that even outsiders had this
impression of Jesus by reputation. Although Herod could
easily have seized Jesus, imprisoned or killed him, (as he did
the Baptist), he never did so, perhaps because he did not
take him that seriously. When Jesus was brought before
Pilate, the Roman governor sent him to Herod:

> When Herod saw Jesus, he was very glad, for he had long
> desired to see him, because he had heard about him; and
> he was hoping to see some sign done by him. So he
> questioned him at some length; but he made no answer.
> The chief priests and scribes stood by, vehemently accus-
> ing him. (23:8-10)

It would seem that Herod was so glad to see Jesus because
he was looking forward to some kind of amusement,
because of news he had heard about him. The king appears
not to have taken seriously the accusations of the chief
priests and scribes. Jesus, however, did not wish to assume
the expected role of a court jester and made no answer. The
text then notes,

> Herod and his soldiers treated him with contempt and
> mocked him; then, arraying him in a gorgeous apparel, he
> sent him back to Pilate. (23:12)

The garment may have been a type of fool's robe, for it
went along with the mocking actions of Herod and his
soldiers. Pilate seems to have agreed with Herod's estimate
of Jesus, for the gospel notes that they became friends as a
result of this agreement (23:12). Pilate also seemed convinced of Jesus' innocence and did not appear to take him
seriously, intending to give him a warning punishment and
let him go (23:13-16).

Compared to that of John at the Jordan, Jesus' approach became so strikingly different that it made him look like a clown in contrast. Jesus respected John as the very finest of a long line of prophets: "I tell you, among those born of women, none is greater than John" (7:28). The Baptist represented the best of the old age and prophetic tradition. When he preached to the crowds, "Repent!" they could see that he took it most seriously in his own life. Repentance was traditionally connected with exterior signs, such as fasting and mortification which were very evident in the Baptist's life-style and appearance. The angel Gabriel had directed his parents to have him follow the Nazarite vow right from the day of his birth. Abstention from alcohol in any form was part of this: "he shall drink no wine or strong drink" (1:15). Another part of the vow was that no scissors or razor should touch the head or beard. (Numbers 6:1-8) The usual vow was for a limited amount of time. John's was life-long.

John must have presented an austere figure of repentance with his untamed beard sweeping over his chest and his long uncut hair draping his shoulders. In addition, his body was thin and gaunt due to frequent fasting. Jesus once said of him, "John the Baptist has come eating no bread and drinking no wine" (7:33). If we take in account Mark 1:6 (one of Luke's sources) it would appear that John was also a vegetarian: his food was "locusts and wild honey" Locusts were not considered as meat. As a vegetarian, John would be following the strictest intrepretation of Scripture, where in the creation account God directs both animals and human beings to eat only green plants and fruits (Genesis 1:29-30). The simplicity of his garb—camel's hair bound about his body with a leather belt—would complete the picture of a stern ascetic whose appearance preached repentance even more than his words.

While John welcomed all who came to him at the Jordan, he was surrounded by a group of male disciples who helped him in his preaching ministry and especially imitated his life-style, becoming in many ways images of their great teacher. Luke notes that many people remarked to Jeus that, "the disciples of John fast often and offer prayers" (5:33). These prayers would be special forms of spiritual and ascetic practices that John taught his disciples.

Jesus remained for a time—we do not know how long—as a colleague[16] of John, baptizing and preaching to those who came to the Jordan. After a time, if we can follow John's gospel (3:23), Jesus moved to a new locality with some disciples but continued the same ministry as John. As far as we know, he at first adopted basically the same approach as John. However, the imprisonment of John by Herod—with the prospect of consequent death—may have been the event that prompted Jesus to rethink his whole ministry. Both Matthew 4:12-17 and Mark 1:14-15 connect the beginning of a new itinerant ministry in Galilee with the news of the Baptist's imprisonment.

The motives for this change are hidden from us, but some factors can be noted. The fate of the Baptist might soon become Jesus' own as well. The time was short and it was important to reach as many people as possible. To do so, Jesus would have to mingle with people and reach them where they were, not wait for the slow process of their arrival at the Jordan. Secondly, Jesus had a secret inner experience of the Spirit at his own baptism that deeply moved him to look in new directions. Somehow the outer trappings of asceticism and fasting that John taught his disciples were too restrictive and confining. John's approach was sincere and devout but obviously meant for a select few male disciples at the Jordan and not for the ordinary person in daily life. There was too much of the old still in it; the New Age had to be *new*, exciting and different.

---

[16]John's gospel appears to be directed against sectarians who claimed to be disciples of the Baptist. (cf. R.E. Brown, *The Gospel According to John I-XII* (Garden City, Doubleday, 1966) pp. LXVII-LXX. Yet despite this, only John retains much material about Jesus and the Baptist that would not help the author's arguments against the Baptist's disciples. E.g., Jesus obtains his first followers from among the followers of John (1:35-51). Jesus baptizes in Judea along with his disciples, at the same time and perhaps close to where John is baptizing (3:22). The simultaneous baptizing ministry of John and Jesus is also noted in 4:1-3. At this point it is said that only Jesus' disciples baptized, not Jesus, but this may be an editorial correction to avoid the close similarity between Jesus and the Baptist.

Had not God said, "Henceforth, I will make you hear new things?" (Isa. 48:6). If Jesus' experience of the Spirit was deeply significant, it would certainly move him in new directions.

A third factor may have been the influence of the Wisdom Tradition on Jesus. Luke give special attention to this in his gospel. Even in the account of Jesus' childhood, the gospel notes his growth in wisdom on two occasions (2:40,52). Other references to wisdom motifs may be found in 7:35; 10:22-23; 20:50. In comparison to the prophetic tradition, the wisdom movement was more open to God's manifestation in all the human experience. The model of the wise person was the young king Solomon. God had revealed himself to the king in a dream promising whatever he would ask. Solomon asked for wisdom in terms (literally) of a "listening heart" so he could give prudent decisions to his people (1 Kings 3:4-15). The broad aspects of wisdom resulting from a "listening heart" are outlined in 5:29-34 where among other things it is noted that God gave Solomon immense wisdom and understanding and a heart as broad as the sand on the seashore, that he composed three thousand proverbs and wrote one thousand and five songs; he could talk about plants, trees, flowers, birds, reptiles, animals and fish; people from all over the world and delegates of kings came to hear his wisdom.

Jesus was very familiar with these legends. One one occasion he recalled the story of the visit of the Queen of Sheba to Solomon and remarked, "A greater than Solomon is here" (Luke 11:31). Jesus was fond of wisdom proverbs and repeated them often; he liked their sense of humor and their keen understanding of human nature brought out through paradoxes and riddles. He must have felt that his greatest gift, like Solomon would be a "listening heart." Such a heart could not remain confined near the Jordan River, but must go out and mingle with people on city streets or on their farms in order to be one with them in their joys, sorrows and daily experiences. Women, children, old and young people, the sick and poor had to be close to him, not the narrow "man's world" of John's daily companions.

Consequently, Jesus decided to begin a new apostolate that had never before been used by a teacher in Israel. He would go out to people wherever he found them, whoever they were and invite them to be his disciples. It did not matter whether they were men or women, Pharisees, tax collectors or sinners, ritually clean or unclean. They were all equal before God and called into the new kingdom of God.

In contrast, the Pharisees were so careful about the laws of table fellowship, that they waited for proof of perfect observance of the Torah before admitting new members. The Scribes and Teachers waited for people to come and humbly ask them for instruction. The pious community of Jewish "monks" (often called the Qumran community) who lived near the Dead Sea welcomed those who came with a commitment to perfectly keep the Torah, but only received them into the community after a long probation period. John the Baptist had taken a giant step forward in welcoming even tax collectors who came to the Jordan, but Jesus would even visit them at their offices (5:27). Women could make a brief visit to the Jordan for repentance and baptism, but could never have stayed in the Baptist's male enclave. Jesus welcomed women to full discipleship and to even accompany him on his journeys (8:1-3).

Along with this change came also a marked difference in attitude toward the solemn and gloomy externals that went along with repentance. Unlike the Baptist, Jesus drank wine and alcohol at the homes and "taverns" of the day. The sad signs of fasting - a practice of the Baptist - (5:33) were discarded. If his disciples did fast on special occasions, it was to be in such a joyful and disguised manner that people would think they were feasting rather than fasting (Matt. 6:16-18). The whole serious atmosphere of religion was to be changed into something playful and joyful.

This complete changeover was a complete shock to most of the Scribes and Pharisees. They could not take him seriously as a teacher of religion. When Jesus ate with tax collectors and sinners, they murmured about him and asked his disciples, "Why do you eat and drink with tax collectors?" (5:31) Even John the Baptist's disciples were surprised at this contrast and questioned Jesus about the lack of fasting among his disciples (5:33; cf. Matt. 9:14, where the question is from the Baptist's disciples.) Even John the Baptist in prison may have been scandalized, for he sent two disciples from prison to ask Jesus whether he was the one to come, or whether they should look for someone else (7:18-19).

Jesus saw his own contrast to the Baptist and Pharisees with a great sense of humor. The difference between the two was like that between a dirge and a dance. The reaction of people was like that of children at play who call to one another in the market place and say, "We piped to you and you did not dance; we wailed and you did now weep"(7:32). Many people looked at himself and the Baptist as representing two ridiculous extremes. Jesus said,

> John the Baptist has come eating no bread and drinking no wine; and you say, "He has a demon." The Son of Man has come eating and drinking; and you say, "Behold a glutton and a drunkard, a friend of tax collectors and sinners." (7:31-35)

Jesus explained the basis of his new life style on one occasion when he was put on the spot and asked why there was such a contrast between the ascetic practices of the Baptist's and Pharisees's disciples and his own: "The disciples of John fast often and offer prayers, and so do the Pharisees, but yours eat and drink" (5:33). Jesus replied with an absolutely ridiculous contrast: "Can you make wedding guests fast while the bridegroom is with them?" (5:34) In other words, religion in the New Age was like a wedding feast, the most joyous occasion in Jewish life. It was celebrated for seven full days with all the food and drink the invited guests desired. There was music, dancing and games for all. All work, unless absolutely necessary, was put aside. It was such a unique occasion that it was the only time in life when the bridal party was excused from the positive obligations of the Torah (prayer, observances, etc.). In likening himself to a bridegroom, Jesus was effectively saying that his approach changed the ordinary somber picture of religion and religion teachers to the most joyous images of human life. The best way to know God would be to follow the wisdom tradition and live life to its fullest with all its beauty, joy and wonder.

Jesus stressed the element of joyful newness in two other images. He said that his way was not just a patched-up fine old suit (previous religious practices) but a complete new suit of clothes (5:36-37). His approach is a sparkling new wine, full of energy, that simply cannot be contained in old dried-out wineskins. In Luke's gospel, Jesus adds another humorous touch: "No one after drinking old wine desires new; for he says, "the old is *better*" (according to a more probable reading).

The title of our chapter, "The Stern Baptist and the Nazarene clown" can now be seen not as an exaggeration but as an understatement. Luke preserves this paradox because it continues to be especially meaningful with the ever-present tendency of religion to return to a set of duties and obligations presided over by solemn and dour teachers, rather than a wedding feast for all with a happy bridegroom leading the festivities.

4

Miracles and Comic Reversals

It is a humorous paradox when the "included" become the excluded; the "excluded," the included; when the "unclean" become the clean and the "clean," the unclean. A good example of this was Jesus' cures on the Sabbath. The holy Sabbath was holy because God made it so by his "example" as taught in the book of Genesis: "God blessed the seventh day and made it holy, because on that day he had rested after all his work or creation" (2:3). The third commandment made it a special day of remembrance:

> For six days you shall labor and do all your work, but the seventh day is a sabbath for the Lord your God. You shall do no work that day, neither you, nor your son nor your daughter nor your servants, men or women nor your animals nor the stranger who lives with you. (Ex. 20:8-10)

The center of Jewish worship was the weekly Sabbath and its remembrance of God's covenant with his people. It began Friday at sunset with a special ritual meal and concluded on Saturday at dusk. It was customary for most Jews to attend the synagogue on Sabbath. There they listened to readings from the Scriptures, followed by a sermon by a teacher and concluded by special prayers. The synagogue became a sacred place for worship. A holy ark in front of the synagogue held the Scriptures, God's sacred writings, which were given special veneration. Jesus was devoted to both Sabbath and synagogue and gave them a special place in his teaching.

However it was a great surprise to all to see Jesus initiate the great action of God *outside* the Holy Sabbath and Sacred Synagogue. Sunset on Saturday night marked the end of the solemn observances. Luke writes,

> Now when the sun was setting, all those who had any that were sick with various diseases brought them to him; and he laid his hands on every one of them and healed them. (4:40)

This took place after the closing of the Sabbath at sunset because it was forbidden to carry burdens on the Sabbath, and many were too ill to come on their own power. Consequently, the ceremonies of the sacred synagogue were of no help to them. Others who were well enough to walk were legally "unclean" because their diseases made them lack the proper wholeness according to the Law that was necessary to take part in such assemblies. In addition, the Sabbath rest meant that all work unless absolutely necessary had to be curtained. Consequently the sick often had less care on the Sabbath than other days. This was especially true of the healing anointments by which the sick were helped in those days. Preparation of such ointments was a forbidden work on the Sabbath.

Jesus healed each one of them by his personal and caring touch: the excluded on the Sabbath became the joy-filled included of God instead of many who sat in the synagogue with somber faces and considered themselves God's included. Jesus did not go out of his way to cure on the Sabbath, but yielded on occasion when pressed to do so. He even found it quite humorous that some people could get so upset about it and yet considered so many other things necessary. Luke mentions three cures on the Sabbath (6:6-11; 14:1-6; 13:10-17). This last will serve as an example of the humorous paradox that Jesus noticed so frequently.

On one occasion when Jesus was preaching on the Sabbath, a woman was present who had been stooped over for eighteen years. Jesus laid his hands on her and cured her so that she stood up straight and praised God. The ruler of the synagogue was indignant and said, "There are six days on which work ought to be done; come on those days and be healed, not on the Sabbath." Jesus answered him,

> You hypocrites! Does not each of you on the Sabbath untie his ox or his ass from the manger and lead it away to water it? And ought not this woman, a daughter of Abraham whom Satan bound for eighteen years be loosed from this bond on the Sabbath day? (13:15-16)

The people of course understood Jesus' joke. Not to cure the woman would be to admit that an ox or ass was more important, and their need for a drink of water was more significant than the woman's 18 year pain. Luke notes the people's reaction: "All the people rejoiced at all the glorious things done by him" (13:17).

Jesus' work for the excluded is especially manifest in his miracles. The selection made by the gospel writers is first of all based on a deliberate parallel to the great works of God in the Old Testament. Secondly, they are selected as examples of Jesus' dramatic reversal of the fate of those who felt themselves most excluded and outcasts from the community of Israel. The most desperate and impossible case was that of the leper. Most of chapters 14 and 15 of Leviticus contain regulations about skin diseases. Once examined and pronounced unclean by the priest, those with serious diseases had to wear torn clothes, leave their hair uncombed, cover their mouths with cloths, and call out "unclean, unclean" so no one would come near them. They dwelt away from any homes, outside the city, often in cemeteries (Lev. 13:45). Such a person was indeed a social and religious outcast who could take part in no ordinary human activities or gatherings.

Official religion was more an obstacle than a help to such people. Such afflicted people could come to the Temple priest not for a cure but certification they were either "clean" or "unclean." If pronounced unclean, that meant a prohibition from religious assemblies in the Temple and synagogue, as well as the social separation already mentioned. Their care then became almost impossible since such ritual uncleanness was often considered contagious and of course there was a dreadful fear of incurring the disease. Therefore no one would touch them to apply healing ointments or give the loving care that would lead to recovery.

We can see then, why Luke only needs a few words to tell the story of a leper's cure, since it is charged with so much underlying emotion:

> While he was in one of the cities, there came a man full of leprosy; and when he saw Jesus, he fell on his face and besought him, "Lord, if you will, you can make me clean." And he stretched out his hand, and touched him, saying, "I will; be clean." And immediately the leprosy left him. (5:12-14)

In touching the leper, Jesus did what no other person would have done for fear of both contagion and ritual uncleanness. The intent of the cure is shown by Jesus' directions that he show himself to the priest and offer the elaborate sacrifices and ritual cleansings necessary for certification as clean. Only then could he take his part once more in community life (5:14). The situation of the leper was of course tragic, but Jesus saw the ridiculous contrast. Official religion and many religious people, lacking real compassion and help for the unfortunate leper, were showing that they were the "unclean" ones in God's sight and not the leper. Jesus must have smiled at least to himself at the paradox: the unclean became clean; and the clean, unclean.

A second cure is even more dramatic than the previous because the woman involved (unlike the leper) had a secret ailment not apparent to others. She had an issue of blood outside the normal menstrual periods. Even during normal times, such a condition imposed upon a woman a ritual uncleanness for seven days. The biblical law considered this uncleanness so contagious that any person she touched became unclean. Even touching utensils or furniture she had previously used had the same effect (Lev. 15:19-24). The woman in the gospel story (8:40-48) was perpetually unclean. Like a leper, if the ailment ever ceased, a special purification rite had to be performed by a temple priest so she could be legally "clean" once more (Lev. 15:28-30).

It is hard to imagine the continual emotional and psychological pain of such a woman who could never touch anyone, or be touched herself for fear of "contagion." She had to be always absent from social and religious gatherings which were prohibited to her. Luke's account tells us simply:

> A woman who had had a flow of blood for twelve years and could not be healed by anyone, came up behind him, and touched the fringe of his garment; and immediately her flow of blood ceased. (8:43-44)

Her unusual mode of action, sneaking up secretly behind Jesus, was taken out of fear that she be recognized and kept from approaching the Master. Luke makes a special point of describing the outcome of the incident. Jesus asked who had touched him and Peter hinted that this was a silly question in view of the crowds pressing around him. The woman, however, with fear and trembling gave public testimony to what had happened:

> In the presence of all the people she declared why she had touched him and how she had been immediately healed. (8:47)

Then he (Jesus) said to her, "Daughter, your faith has made you well; go in peace." The extreme paradox in the story must have been evident to all. Here was a woman singled out for 12 years for public exclusion. Doctors could not help her; religion made it worse by making her legally unclean as well. She was not "whole" and thus her physical ailment was commonly regarded as the result of secret sins. Jesus, however, singled her out from the excluding crowd. She then became the one most included in God's blessings as the result of her deep faith and trusting touch of Jesus' garment. It was another comic reversal of the New Age in which the unclean become clean and the excluded the included.

A final example to which Luke attaches a great deal of importance is the cure of the paralytic. Usually Luke's miracle stories are considerably shorter than those of Mark. However, in this case Luke is longer than Mark and Matthew. These latter writers report the presence of Scribes on the occasion (Mark 1:6; Matt 9:9), but Luke adds Pharisees to their number and notes also that they had come "from every village of Galilee and Judea and from Jerusalem" (5:17). It appears that our author is setting the stage for a very important teaching.

Jesus was teaching at his adopted home in Capernaum, where so many people were gathered, even outside the door, that no one else could possibly enter. Forced by this situation, four men carrying a paralytic on a bed climbed up the roof of the house, made an opening in it and let the man down on ropes to set him before Jesus. The Master was struck by the faith shown in their unusual feat. He said to the paralyzed person, "Man, your sins are forgiven you." (5:20) Luke notes the shock and reactions of the teachers who were critical observers of the whole situation:

> The Scribes and the Pharisees began to question, saying, "Who is this that speaks blasphemies? Who can forgive sins but God only?" (5:21)

Their serious questioning was probably due to a combination of three reasons. First of all, only God in heaven could pronounce a human being to be forgiven from sin. Secondly this was to be expected in the great age to come; only then would God freely forgive all sins (e.g. Jer. 31:33-

34; Ez. 36:25-29; Zech. 13:10). Preparation for such a boun-
tiful forgiveness should be made by the perfect observance
of the Torah to which these teachers had devoted their lives.
Forgiveness had to be earned and first given to those who
best deserved it.

In contrast, Jesus by a simple, unexpected word had
assured God's forgiveness to a man who was obviously a
sinner in people's eyes since he was being punished by so
serious an affliction. How could anyone take Jesus' word
seriously? Luke carefully provides a basis for Jesus' unusual
statement. First of all he introduces the passage by writing
that Jesus had the power of the Lord with him to hear (5:17).
In other words, Jesus' word was the healing word of God.
Secondly, this healing word is able to cure the whole person,
interiorly and exteriorly. Hence Jesus is able to say, "That
you may know that the Son of Man has power on earth to
forgive sins,"—I say to you, "rise, take up your bed and go
home." The third basis is Luke's own experience in the early
church where he sees abundant forgiveness within the community as a result of the presence of this risen Son of Man.

The radical contrast between Jesus' critical observers and
this warm, total forgiveness and cure is not lost on the
audience. They exclaim, "We have seen strange things
today" (5:26). The translation, "strange things" is from the
Greek *paradoxa* from which we get "paradox " in English.
Jesus' action is paradox at its best: the future last times
become present. The unforgiven becomes the forgiven; the
unearned becomes the earned. Those who think they have
earned find themselves as mere spectators, left out of the
process.

Luke is so interested in the stories of Jesus' miracles
because he has found the same paradox in the healings in the
early church through Jesus' name and presence. G.
O'Toole[17] has pointed out in the continuity between Jesus'
miracles in the gospel and those in Acts. Jesus cures Peter's
mother-in-law's fever (Lk 4:38-39), while Paul does almost

---

[17] *The Unity of Luke's Theology*, p. 239

the same for Publius' father who was sick with fever and dysentery (Acts 28:8). Just as Jesus cured the paralytic in the story, so Peter and Paul both heal paralytics (Acts 3:1-10; 9:32-35; 14:8-10). Similar summary statements of the Apostles' healing resemble those about Jesus (Peter, Acts 5:15-16; Paul, Acts 19:11-12).

A striking example of this parallel is found in the cure of a paralytic by Peter and John at the gate of the Temple. Luke gives a detailed description of this to show that the remarkable paradox of Jesus' healings continues in the church as a result of the presence of the risen Lord.

> Now Peter and John were going up to the temple at the hour of prayer, the ninth hour. And a man lame from birth was being carried, whom they laid daily at that gate of the temple which is called Beautiful to ask alms of those who entered the temple. Seeing Peter and John about to go into the temple, he asked for alms. (Acts 3:1-3)

The contrast pictured in this scene could hardly be more extreme. The temple was the center of institutional religion. This man had spent almost a life-time sitting helpless at the Temple gate. Thousands of priests and holy levites had passed him by, offering a few coins but unable to give him what he really wanted. Countless sacrifices had been offered at the altar of holocausts but they offered him no glimmer of hope. His affliction was deep seated, a deformity from birth that most people consider to be caused by sins of his parents. This day was just one more day of humiliation and suffering as he was carried by family or friends to take his accustomed place by the temple gate. He could never, of course, be brought into the temple area itself, because such afflictions disqualified his possibility of admittance. As Peter and John were about to enter, the lame beggar stretched out his hand and asked for alms.

Every detail in Luke's story is significant: "Peter directed his gaze at him, with John, and said, 'Look at us'" (3:4). Here they imitate the Master whose full gaze and attention meant that God's power was to work through him (e.g. Lk 22:61). Peter then said, "I have no silver and gold, but I give you what I have; in the name of Jesus Christ of Nazareth, walk. Then Peter took him by the right hand, raised him up and immediately his feet and ankles became strong (3:6-7). The use of the name of Jesus signified that the apostles were but instruments of the continued presence and healing power of Jesus of Nazareth. G. O'Toole[17] draws attention to Luke's strong emphasis on joy and praise: the man leaps and jumps with joy, praising God. Now he enters the temple area *with* Peter and John, something he had never been able to do in all his life. The people recognize him as former helpless paralytic beggar at the Temple gate. They in turn are filled with wonder and amazement (ekstasis) at what has happened to him (3:8-10).

Peter then addressed the people and affirmed that it was not their power or holiness that affected the cure: "Men of Israel, why do you wonder at this, or why do you stare at us, as though by our own power or piety we hade made him walk?" He then told the story of Jesus' death and resurrection and repeated that it is *his name* that has brought about the extraordinary miracle: "His name, by faith in his name, has made this man strong whom you see and know; and the faith which is through Jesus has given the man this perfect health in the presence of you all (3:13-16). The name, signifying the continued presence and power of Jesus was so important that Peter called attention to this a third time after his arrest and during a trial before the high priest; Luke describes Peter as full of the Holy Spirit when he utters these words:

> If we are being examined today concerning a good deed done to a cripple, by what means this man has been healed, be it known to you all, and to all the people of Israel, that by the name of Jesus Christ of Nazareth, whom you crucified, whom God raised from the dead, by him this man is standing before you well. (4:8-10)

Luke is very conscious of the reactions that many people

would have in attributing the apostles' work to some special type of magic or deceit. Indeed, the same reactions occur today. He is anxious to show that the use of the name of Jesus is not a magical formula but a direct way of bringing the presence and power of Jesus of Nazareth to bear on the desperate situation and thus continue the paradoxical surprise of Jesus' miracles among his own people in Israel. Luke illustrates the difference between magic formulas and faith in Jesus' presence by one of the most humorous stories in the bible.

Paul, like Peter and John, had used the name of Jesus in healings and exorcisms. This fact was observed by some Jewish exorcists who thought it to be a magic formula they also could use. These exorcists were prominent Jews, the seven sons of a Jewish high priest named Sceva. They were especially looked up to by the ordinary people because of their association with the holiest functions of the Temple. These men started to also use the name of Jesus, as if it were a magical formula. Luke must have had a smile on his face as he wrote these words:

> The evil spirit answered them, 'Jesus I know, and Paul I know; but who are you?' And the man in whom the evil spirit was leaped on them, mastered all of them, and overpowered them, so that they fled out of that house naked and wounded. (Acts 19:15-16)

The significance of this striking incident was not lost among the people of Ephesus: "The *name* of the Lord Jesus was extolled" (19:17). Not only that, but many Christians who still adhered to magical practices confessed what they had done, brought out their books of magic and burnt them (19:18-19). Luke even points out that the worth of the books burned was fifty thousand pieces of silver! (19:19).

5

Feasts of Fools

A common picture of the New Age was that of a great banquet feast prepared by God for the just. For example, the prophet Isaiah describes a future great victory banquet of Israel in these words:

> On this mountain the Lord of hosts will make for all people a feast of fat things, a feast of wine on the lees, of fat things full of marrow, of wine on the lees well refined. (25:6)

It would be quite natural for Scribes and Pharisees as teachers of Israel to picture themselves as presiding over such a meal accompanied by their fervent disciples. It would be a great feast in an illumined banquet hall with sinners, tax collectors, and those not zealous for the Torah consigned to the darkness outside, moaning their miserable fate.

Luke sees Jesus as reversing this scene. The book of Proverbs described a banquet of fools as a contrast to the banquet of the just (9:1-18). However, our evangelist protrays banquet scenes where those reputed as "fools," in the sense of being excluded, find themselves included in God's banquet, and those who considered themselves as included, find themselves outside. These "fools" would include tax collectors, sinners, the unclean, the unfortunate, handicapped, the sick and the mentally afflicted. These last groups were often considered possessed by devils or judged as being punished for secret sins. It is these people who will be part of a great comic reversal in a "feast of fools" where they are the especially beloved of God.

The first of such scenes in Luke is that of the great banquet of Levi the tax collector. Levi was a Jewish tax collector who had his office by the sea of Galilee, perhaps near Capernaum. Men such as he were usually rich, since the office had to be bought at a great price from the Romans or from Herod. Among most people there was a natural antipathy for Romans as foreign oppressors. But this was nothing compared to their hatred of a fellow Jew who cooperated in the oppression of the poor through heavy taxation. In addition, the average tax collector was suspected of cheating when he could, collecting much more than was appointed to him. They were regarded as unclean because of their association with foreigners and considered sinners as well. The fervent observers of the law would not associate with them or take meals with them.

When Jesus spoke of loving one's enemies, the first person most people thought of was the despised, avaricious tax collector. We can imagine what a surprise it was to everyone when Jesus singled out Levi and chose him to be a member of his close circle of disciples. The gospels are silent on what must have been the shock of the other disciples of Jesus when they found themselves side by side with the same Levi who had so often collected their last pennies at his tax office!

Luke highlights the scene by writing that "Levi made him a great feast in his house" (5:29a). Here Levi is the host of the celebration while in Matthew 9:10 and Mark 2:15, it appears to be at the house of Jesus. "There was a large company of tax collectors and others sitting at table with him" (5:29b). These "others" are called "sinners" in the next verse by the Pharisees. The word "sinner" was used not only of wrongdoers, but even of those whose profession or work offered considerable temptation to wrongdoing or made it difficult

for them to observe the Torah. Thus merchants, shopkeep-
ers, shepherds, and women who offered hospitality as
innkeepers, were often referred to in this manner.

A feast hosted by Levi with the presence of such people
would surely be avoided by the "just," who could not break
the laws of table fellowship which prohibited eating foods
prepared by foreigners or the lawless. We can understand
why the Pharisees murmured and questioned Jesus' disciples, "Why do you eat and drink with tax collectors and
sinners?" (5:30) Jesus' answer provides the humorous
paradox,

> Those who are well have no need of a physician but those
> who are sick; I have not come to call the righteous, but
> sinners to repentance. (5:31-32)

In other words, the banquet of "fools and sinners" who
know they need forgiveness is the banquet of those included
by Jesus the Physician, for only these people can profit from
his healing power. In contrast, the banquet of the "wise and
just" who do not feel this need is really the banquet of fools,
who have excluded themselves.

The contrast is even further emphasized in the story of the
call of Zacchaeus the rich head tax collector of Jericho,
found only in Luke:

> He sought to see who Jesus was, but could not on account
> of the crowd because he was small of stature. So he ran on
> ahead and climbed up into a sycamore tree to see him, for
> he was to pass that way. (19:3-4)

The story seems to have some double meanings. Zacchaeus is small of stature not only externally but internally.
He realizes his need and tries to overcome it by taking the
risk of appearing foolish enough to climb a tree in order to
see Jesus. There must certainly have been a smile on Jesus'
face when he looked up into the tree and said to him,
"Zacchaeus, make haste and come down; for I must stay at
your house today." The tax collector hastened to come

down and welcomed Jesus joyfully into the house. However, almost everyone was upset by this: "When they saw it, they all murmured, "'he has gone in to be the guest of a man who is a sinner.'" What they did not see was that the banquet of God is not made possible by the "just" inviting God but by God inviting (here through Jesus) those sinners who really need and want him. This is what makes the banquet so joyful.

The banquet theme in Luke is further strengthened by a collection of three dinner parables found in 14:7-24. The first story comes by way of observation on the way people invited to a banquet ususally struggle to get the best places of honor near the host or important people. Jesus, however, sees the comedy and contrast to God's banquet:

> When you are invited by any one to a marriage feast, do not sit in a place of honor, lest a more eminent person than you be invited by him; and he who invited you both will come and say to you, "Give place to this person" and then you will begin with shame to take the lowest place. (14:8-9)

The key to the humorous contrast is found in the verb "invite" repeated eight times in 14:7-14. In the kingdom, to be invited by God is the supreme privilege of life. Those who understand this are overwhelmed with joy, realizing their own unworthiness and inability to earn this in any way. Those who forget this and push their way forget the grace that brought them there and end up in the lowest place. Their trust in power brings about their downfall. On the contrary,

> When you are *invited*, go and sit in the lowest place, so that when your host comes he may say to you, 'Friend, go up higher'; then you will be honored in the presence of all who sit at table with you. (14:10)

Here to the contrary, those who joyously accept the invitation, choose the most humble seat and renounce power find themselves unexpectedly raised up to a place of honor. This leads to Jesus' comic punchline: "For everyone who exalts himself will be humbled" (14:11). This is so unlike ordinary human experience that Jesus' paradox and joke always remains.

The cue word "invite" leads to another teaching of Jesus:

> He said also to the man who had invited him "When you give a dinner or banquet, do not invite your friends or your brothers or your kinsmen or rich neighbors, lest they also invite you in return, and you be repaid. But when you give a feast, invite the poor, the maimed, the lame, the blind and you will be blessed because they cannot repay you. You will be repaid at the resurrection of the just. (14:12-14)

Once again the word "invite" provides the key to a ridiculous contrast. A true banquet invitation is characterized by pure grace which has no expectations attached. It is once again a "feast of fools" by earthly standards. Present are the great hordes of the excluded, especially the poor and the handicapped. These latter, the maimed, the blind and lame were excluded from the Temple because of their lack of physical integrity, often assumed to be joined to a deficiency of moral integrity. In contrast, an invitation to special friends, relatives and rich neighbors is often more like an investment with guaranteed returns. It pays off well in life, so why is God needed at all?

These last two parables are only in Luke. Because these and many other stories are only handed down by him, it has sometimes been questioned whether they belong to the historical Jesus. I suppose Luke might answer that he did not consider himself a mechanical transfer agent of the exact words of Jesus' sayings and stories. The real historical Jesus presented a paradox in his sayings and life style. When that paradox comes to life again in a new situation, then people find out what Jesus really meant. For today, Luke might say that a church or community has found Jesus where the handicapped and poor have the first place in everyone's hearts along with practical application.

The third banquet parable is parallel to Matthew 22:1-10. They may both be from the common sayings source "Q", those parts of Matthew and Luke that are not in Mark but shared by these two authors. However, the account in Luke has some remarkable differences. This is perhaps due to Luke's desire to come in contact with the Master by retaining the permanent paradox in his teaching for all time. The context is the statement of a man who heard the first two parables and exclaimed, "Blessed is he who shall eat bread in the kingdom of God" (14:15). This shows that Luke's interest moves toward God's great future banquet and its characteristics. Matthew is concerned more with the situation of the Jewish people in regard to Jesus: "The kingdom of heaven may be compared to a king who gave a marriage feast for his son" (Matt. 22:2). Luke, however, immediately broadens the perspective to a wider audience, "A man once gave a great banquet, and invited many." Such a banquet invitation especially as in Matthew, a wedding feast for a king's son, was the privilege of a life-time. However, it meant a total commitment of time to accept the invitation. Even an ordinary wedding meant seven full days of celebration, leaving all work and ordinary activities. A king's son's wedding would mean a much greater commitment.

In the parable, many wise and calculating people made excuses, and they were important ones. One had bought some property and had to inspect it; another had made the enormous investment of buying five oxen and was anxious to try them out. A third had just married and wished to enjoy his life as a newlywed. This last was regarded so seriously in tradition that newlywed husbands were exempt from military duty even in a Holy War (Deut. 20:7). The master in the story was disappointed and even angry at their refusal. No specific punishment is named as in Matthew 22:7; perhaps their absence from the great banquet is punishment enough in itself. However, the anger of the host is only momentary and prompts him to become even more generous in the scope of his invitations:

He said to his servant, "Go out quickly to the streets and

lanes of the city and bring in the poor and maimed and
blind and lame. (14:21)

This group, who already appeared in the last parable, are
not "wise" and calculating as the first group, who refused to
risk anything of their own. These poor and handicapped
were the "foolish" who were overwhelmed with joy at such
an unexpected and gracious invitation. Consequently, they
ignored the risks involved. Actually they were already the
great excluded ones from religion and society. Once again
the great banquet becomes a "feast of fools," in contrast to
the "wise" who become excluded and foolish. The parable
then continues,

> The servant said, 'Sir, what you commanded has been
> done, and still there is room.' And the master said to the
> servant, 'Go out to the highways and hedges, and compel
> people to come in, that my house may be filled.' (14:23)

We see that the bounty of the host is never exhausted. In
fact the extent of his hospitality appears as foolish as that of
a person who would use the entire phone book address list
to invite people to a dinner. The missionary command is to
go out to the entire earth—the "foolish" unclean Gentile
world, excluded from Israel. The words, "Compel people to
come in," do not imply force but belong to the terminology
and customs of oriental hospitality which does not easily
take "no" for an answer. The expression, "That my house
may be filled," sums up the purpose of the master: the great
final banquet of God is not meant for a few privileged "just"
with a hall of many empty seats. It is meant to be literally a
full house with every seat filled with the excluded, the
"foolish," the handicapped and the vast unclean multitudes.
Once again Luke records these things because he has
experienced the paradox of Jesus' words in his own life. He
has seen the unclean become the clean and the excluded
become the included. He has seen people eating together at
table who have never been able to do so in all of world
history. We can establish this because he has written a

second volume called the acts of the Apostles. There he tells the story of Peter, who had previously kept all the rules about clean and unclean food that prevented Jews and Gentiles from enjoying table fellowship. While waiting for dinner one day, Peter had a dream in which he saw a large sheet let down from the sky filled with unclean animals. A voice said to him, "Arise, Peter, Kill and Eat." In horror, Peter replied that he had never done so in his life. The voice then said, "Do not call anything unclean that God has called clean." The whole dream was repeated three times (Acts 10:9-14). While Peter was pondering over this unusual vision, a Roman centurion and his companions appeared at the door. Peter remembered his dream and invited the Gentiles into his house, giving them food and hospitality, something he had never before done in his life. He then went with Cornelius and stayed at his house. The whole matter was such a shock to the Jerusalem Jewish-Christian community when they heard the news that they criticized Peter for disobeying the Jewish Law, saying, "What is this that you entered the house of the uncircumcised and ate with them?" (11:3)

For the same reason, Luke makes a special point of writing about the very first time that a combined Jewish and Gentile community appeared at Antioch. (Acts 11:20-21) A mixed community such as this was an unheard of phenomenon in world history. It would necessarily entail table fellowship, since Christianity was centered about special meals in remembrance of Jesus. For Luke, the meals between Jews and Gentiles are the continuation of Jesus' feasts of fools with sinners and disadvantaged. This does not mean that all Christians immediately adopted this practice. It was simply too much for some of them, especially those who were Pharisee converts, since the practices of the Pharisees were centered about very strict rules concerning foods and table fellowship.

This reluctance is illustrated in Acts 15, where there was a great meeting of the early church in Jerusalem to discuss questions about requirements for Gentile converts. Some believers, former Pharisees, insisted on circumcision and full observance of the Mosaic law for Gentile converts (15:5). This would have meant obedience to all the laws about foods and table fellowship that had created such a barrier between Jews and Gentiles for hundreds of years. Failure to do so would mean that they could not be equal partners around the same common table. At most they could achieve the status of second class citizens. Peter stood up and insisted that the yoke of the law should not be placed on Gentile believers; the essential matter was the grace of the Lord Jesus (15:10-11). Then James, the leader of the Jewish community at Jerusalem addressed the group proposing a compromise: it was simply abhorrent to Jews to eat meats sacrificed to idols or to eat animals whose blood had not been carefully poured into the ground. The community agreed that Gentiles should respect this, and a letter to surrounding churches was drawn up to circulate their decision. In this way, Luke brings out the Jesus' "feasts for fools" continued to be an extraordinary witness in the early church as both Jews and Gentiles ate together at the same table and shared the same foods. Jesus' words would have become dead to the world unless the original paradox of the "feast of fools" had become a reality in the experience of the early church. In fact they only have meaning today when the paradox comes alive again and again in history.

6

Crazy Discipleship:

The Sermon on the Plain

Both Matthew and Luke draw from a common source the tradition of a Sermon on the Mount (On the Plain, in Luke). Luke's version is much shorter; it omits all references to the bible or Law to make it more applicable to the non-Jewish world. It heightens the paradoxical elements to almost ridiculous extremes. The evangelist's purpose is to show that true discipleship represents such a radical and comical contrast to ordinary people's ways that a disciple of Jesus can easily be recognized. In Luke, Jesus introduces the Sermon with four sharply contrasting beatitudes and woes to bring out this difference.

Blessed are you poor, for yours is the
kingdom of God. Blessed are you who
hunger now for you shall be satisfied.
Blessed are you that weep now, for you
shall laugh. Blessed are you when men hate
you, and when they exclude you and revile
you and cast out your name as evil, on
account of the Son of Man. Rejoice in that

> day, and leap for joy, for behold, your
> reward is great in heaven; (6:20-23)

In direct contrast,

> Woe to you that are rich, for you have re-
> ceived your consolation. Woe to you that are
> full now, for you shall hunger. Woe to you
> that laugh now, for you shall mourn and weep.
> Woe to you, when all men speak well of you for
> so their fathers did to the prophets. (6:24-25)

An important key to the Beatitudes' meaning in Luke is
the strong focus on Jesus' disciples: "He (Jesus) lifted up his
eyes on his *disciples* and spoke" (6:20). What Jesus is about
to say finds meaning in the call of a disciple. Matthew and
Mark have brief accounts of the call of the twelve (4:18-22
and 1:16-20), but Luke has it within the vivid imagery of a
miraculous catch of fish (5:1-11). The emphasis is on Jesus'
word which will enable the disciples to be fishers of human
beings (5:1,5,10). This teaching word accompanies the healing word of Jesus which immediately precedes the Sermon
on the Plain (6:17-19).

This ministry of word and healing will have special priority in the disciples' lives. Matthew and Mark describe Peter,
Andrew, James and John leaving their fishing nets and
home to follow Jesus. Luke pushes this even further and
writes, "They left *everything* and followed him" (5:11). This
commitment to follow Jesus as itinerant preachers and
healers would have dramatic economic consequences for
them. It would mean dependence on other people for food
and hospitality wherever they went and reduction of their
travelling requirements to the bare necessities (9:2-6). At
home, it would mean a drastic decrease of family income to
a minimum, rather than the security and added comforts
made possible by full time work. In reality, Jesus was calling
for a revolution in the use of time.[18] As much time as

---

[18]For a more complete description of this "revolution in the use of time," cf. my
book *Broken Bread and Broken Bodies: The Lord's Supper and World Hunger.*

possible would be used in personal ministry through healing and teaching rather than the usual total absorption in work from dawn to dusk.

The beatitudes are meant to bring out the "ridiculous" consequences of such a commitment to discipleship. Followers of Jesus will be voluntarily poor because of the way they use time, but rich in possessing all they need in God's kingdom. As a result, they will often be hungry, but God will satisfy them. In their sensitivity to human need and suffering, they will weep often, but God will make them laugh with joy. They will be thrown out of cities as well as synagogues and cursed, but they will actually rejoice and even dance with joy because their voluntary suffering will be a beautiful gift to God like that of his beloved prophets.

Luke recovers the paradox in the beatitudes for he has known of it in the early Jerusalem community and experienced it himself as a travelling apostle. In Jerusalem, Christians became poor by choice through their commitment to provide a daily distribution of food and goods to the needy (Acts 6:1). When necessary, many sold houses and property to make this possible (Acts 3:44-45; 4:34-35). In practice, if everyone was to eat, some had to be voluntarily hungry from time to time. The Acts of the Apostles tells the stories of travelling apostles like Philip (8:26-40), Paul and others. Hardly a chapter goes by without one of them being thrown into prison, scorged or humiliated in some way. Their reaction was that of the beatitudes: "Rejoice in that day."

To confirm this, Luke tells the story of Paul and Silas who were whipped, stripped of their clothes and thrown into prison at Philippi. Yet at midnight, the jailors found them praying and singing (Acts 16:22-25). While Luke recognized that every Christian could not be a travelling apostle, he emphasized for everyone the radical priority of the kingdom. Travelling apostles served as models and mentors for their converts in discovering the meaning of discipleship in daily life.

The paradox and humorous contrast in Luke's beatitudes repeats itself constantly when Christians restrict their work and incomes for the same revolution of time needed to personally serve others. As "wasters of time" they draw the laughs of those for whom work, income, security and power is everything in life, but the real laugh of joy comes from living out the paradox of a true disciple.

The rest of the Sermon on the Plain draws its inspiration from imitation of God himself. As such, it is rare and unusual, at times even laughable like the experience of Abraham and Sarah. This is because it seems so impossible and unlike what most people do. The model of imitation of God is found in 6:35-36, "You will be sons of the Most High: for he is kind to the ungrateful and the selfish. Be merciful even as your Father is merciful."

Once again, Luke recovers the paradox in Jesus' words because he was so keenly aware of the striking and even funny contrast between the life style of a disciple and the ordinary Greek person on the streets. Luke himself was probably brought up in the Greek Gentile world. Among the Greeks, the highest virtue was that of friendship. Greek literature is filled with praises and examples of this relationship. The Greek school or *gymnasion* was a place where deep and affectionate relationships were developed between master and disciple as well as between students. Greek philosophical communities prided themselves on being societies of friends. Luke does not criticize this view, but is anxious to show that being a Christian does much more than merely canonize Greek friendship. On the contrary, imitation of God presents a surprising and challenging new model. Luke begins with Jesus' views on the "outsider" or enemy:

> But I say to you that hear, Love your enemies, do good
> to those who hate you, bless those curse you,
> pray for those who abuse you. (6:27-28)

For most people, then as today, toleration of enemies, avoidance of vengeance or just leaving them to God's punishment would be considered a most noble response. However, discipleship as imitation of God goes to "crazy" heights. Special attention and love is to be shown to the outsider and enemy in a most practical way. Luke seems to be putting together a seven-fold list perhaps to contrast it with the "traditional' seven fold vengeance (Gen. 4:15). These may be enumerated as follows:

1) Doing good to hateful enemies, 2) blessing them and 3) praying for them. These are not just noble ideals but points for practice especially for the travelling apostle. For example, Paul a companion of Luke wrote to the Corinthians, "When we are cursed, we respond with a blessing (1 Cor. 4:12). 4) "To him who strikes you on the cheek offer the other also." This seems to illustrate the type of love that is willing to suffer another injury rather than responding in kind. 5) "From him who takes away your cloak do not withold your coat as well." This points to a humorous loving "reprisal" of offering even more to someone who has literally taken the cloak off you back, perhaps through a lawsuit as in the parallel in Matt. 5:40. 6) "Give to everyone who begs of you." This may be a generous cheerful response to someone who is shaming forcing you to respond through insistent, aggressive begging. 7) "Of him who takes away your goods, do not ask them again." Here the act of love counters the natural tendency to demand restitution. Instead the person makes a gift of what had been a robbery. As a final summary, the "golden rule" of identification with another's need covers all cases: "And as you wish that people would do to you, do so to them" (6:31).

The last section (31-35) would be a special contrast to the Greek supreme ideal of friendship, because the latter has certain traits of an investment with a well secured return:

> If you love those who love you, what credit
> is that to you? For even sinners love those
> who love them. And if you do good to those who
> do good to you, what credit is that to you?
> For even sinners do the same (6:32-33).

Friendships in the Greek world also offered many practical advantages such as mutual loans and business partnerships. However, Luke wants to show that God's love

mirrored in human beings is on an infinitely superior level.
It reaches out to all without ulterior motivation or the
expectation of any return:

> If you lend to those from whom you hope to re-
> ceive, what credit is that to you? Even sinners
> lend to sinners, to receive as much again. But love
> your enemies, and do good, and lend expecting
> nothing in return; and your reward will be very great,
> and you will be sons of the most High; for he is
> kind to the ungrateful and the selfish. Be merciful even as
> your Father is merciful. (6:34-36)

Jacques Dupont[19] has given considerable study to the
possible influence of the Greek ideal of friendship on Luke.
An ancient Greek axiom, possibly from as far back as
Pythagoras, stated that "among friends everything is common (*koina*)." Perhaps Luke was influenced by this ideal
when he stated in Acts 2:44 that the early believers held
everything in common (*koina*). However, Luke goes far
beyond the reciprocal Greek motifs by stressing that this
sharing took within its scope the most destitute and needy
such as widows (Acts 6:1).

The next section on judging would be extremely important for any group aspiring to embody a divine paradox in
face of the world. Their life style may be a comedy in
contrast, but there can never be the caustic type of humor
that is a veiled judgment of others in dispuise. An illustration may help here. As noted in the introduction, Will
Rogers was a beloved American humorist who died in an air
crash in the middle thirties. He could poke fun at American
institutions, even congress and the President. Yet it was a
kindly sense of humor that invited people to laugh at themselves. No "put downs" were involved. He once said in
regard to his role as a comedian that he never met a person
that he didn't like. According to Luke's portrayal, Jesus as a

---

[19]In his chapter, "Community of Goods in the Early Church," in his book *The
Salvation of the Nations.*

"jokester" was that type of a person. The evangelist invites his readers to follow this model and not take themselves too seriously in comparison with others:

> Judge not, and you will not be judged; condemn not, and you will not be condemned; forgive and you will be forgiven; give, and it will be given to you; good measure, pressed down, shaken together, running over, will be poured into your lap. For the measure you give will be the measure you get back. (6:37-38)

Jesus provided a radical substitute for a judgemental, condemning or criticizing attitude toward others when he said, "forgive and you will be forgiven; give, and it will be given to you. The results of such an attitude would be an unbelievable surprise. Only Luke records Jesus' humorous images at this point. In buying or selling, a long robe was handy for measuring out wheat or grain. A shrewd seller would usually try to give the minimum yet make it look like the maximum by not packing it down. In contrast, Jesus pictures a surprisingly generous transaction with the grain shaken together, pressed down, and even spilling over. Such is the response of people (and of God) to a generous, forgiving and accepting attitude. On the other side, a judgmental and condemnatory attitude is met with reciprocity by others and by God himself.

The whole manner of Christian teaching is very much connected with this. Jesus' main approach to teaching was through example: "follow me" was an invitation to imitation by accompanying him and learning his life style through observation and practice. Early Christianity followed the same model. The Acts of the Apostles shows that the early Christian centers were households where Christian converts lived with their teachers who could show them the new way through their example and lives. Jesus sums this up in a brief parable: "Can a blind man lead a blind man? Will they not both fall into a pit?" (6:39). The new way of life was contagious; therefore the heights reached by the disciple could be no more than the teacher's level before God: "A disciple is not above his teacher, but everyone when he is fully taught will be like his teacher" (6:40).

The great temptation of teachers (and parents!) then as now was to provide continual correction. It is a pitfall because it takes away from personal awareness, honesty and self-correction which is the best way to help others. So we have the well-known humorous observation of Jesus:

> How can you say to your brother, 'Brother, let me
> take out the speck that is in your eye,' when you your-
> self do not see the log that is in your own eye.'
> You hypocrite, first take the log out of your own,
> eye, and then you will see clearly to take out the
> speck that is in your brother's eye. (6:42)

When this directive of Jesus is followed, another paradox results, if we keep in mind verses 37 and 39 about judgment. When we clearly see our own faults and expose them to forgiveness, our sight becomes "blurred." We tend to see faults or "specks" in others as an occasion of love and forgiveness rather than a source of admonitions and criticism. With this in mind, good teachers will be recognized not by knowledge, eloquence or other qualifications, but by their fruits in good lives. It would indeed be a real laugh to expect "figs from a thorn bush, or grapes from brambles" (6:43-44).

> The good person out of the good treasure of
> the heart produces good, and the evil person
> out of an evil treasure produces evil: for out
> of the abundance of the heart of the mouth speaks. (6:4-5)

In other words, not what we *say* but what we *are* really counts. Only Luke records the expression "good treasure of the heart." For him, the heart is the center of feelings and life direction. Luke also emphasizes the heart in the seed parable: the good soil is that which recieves the seed in "an honest and good *heart*" and brings forth fruit with patience (8:15).

7

Is a Woman's Place at Home?

Luke has often been called "the gospel of women." In fact the feminine orientation of this gospel has profoundly affected Christian theology, especially the portrait of Mary the Mother of Jesus. Why was Luke so interested in this side of Jesus' ministry? The answer can be found in the Acts of the Apostles where we discover the notable role of women in the spread of early Christianity. The Greek world that Luke knew was still a man's world dominated by strong patriarchal structures, even though Greek women had considerably more freedom than their more traditionally bound Jewish counterparts. Yet there are many signs that Luke was deeply moved by the feminine initiative and activity he witnessed in the early church. It was a surprising contrast and paradox to the patriarchal Greek world he lived in.

To begin with, the formative beginnings of the Jerusalem church took place in the household of a woman called Mary, mother of John/Mark (Acts 12:12), Luke notes that an important group of women were present at the first Pentecost including Mary, the mother of Jesus (1:14). This house was an important gathering plcae for early Christians, and very probably the location of the upper room of the first Pentecost (1:13; 2:1), the place to which Peter and John returned after prison (4:23,31).

The care of widowed women was an important concern of the early church (6:2). A disciple called Tabitha/Dorcas appears to have been part of a community of widows dedicated to "good works and acts of charity" (9:39,41). When Tabitha became sick and died, the community sent two men for Peter who immediately came and worked a great miracle, raising her to life (9:41). The entry of the gospel into Europe was an important turning point in the early church. It was made possible by a group of women who had gathered together to listen to the apostle Paul at Philippi in Greece at a place of prayer by a river just outside the city. One of their number was Lydia, a prominent woman who headed a large household. She welcomed Paul to her home which became the first Christian church in Europe (16:14-15).

A married couple, Aquila and Priscilla, were key figures in Paul's apostolate. They were already Christians when Paul came to stay at their home in Corinth, which became a Christian meeting place (18:2-3). Priscilla seems to have been the more active of the two since Luke names her first on two occasions (18:18,26). The dedicated couple converted Apollos, an eloquent early Christian preacher (18:24-27). Paul had such confidence in them that he brought them to Ephesus to begin an important apostolate in that city while he himself continued on to Jerusalem (18:19). Paul later sent a special greeting to them as people "to whom not only I but also all the churches of the Gentiles give thanks." He also greeted the church centered at their house (Rom. 16:3-5). Luke draws attention to younger women also and their importance. In Paul's final journey to Jerusalem, he stopped at Caesarea at the house of Philip the Evangelist. Luke notes that Philip had four unmarried daughters who prophesied. (21:8-9).

Why all this stress on women in the early church? Luke may be finding this necessary to bring out the exact fulfilment of God's plan for the last times as announced in the prophet Joel. There God had announced that in age, the Holy Spirit would be manifest in a way t break down the usual barriers of sex, age and class. Luke has Peter quote this prophecy on Pentecost day:

> In the last days, it shall be, God declares
> that I will pour out my Spirit upon all flesh
> and your sons and your daughters shall prophesy
> and your young men shall see visions
> and your old men shall dream dreams
> and on my menservants and my maidservants in those
> days I will pour out my Spirit; and they shall prophesy.
> (Joel 2:28-30; Acts 2:17-18)

Luke feels that the supreme sign of the Spirit is a great universality that brings together male and female (sons and daughters), young and old, even male and female servants. The final result will be, in the words of Joel "that whoever calls on the name of the Lord shall be saved (2:32; Acts 2:21). This is why Luke carefully indicated each group in writing the Acts of the Apostles. However, as he wrote the gospel, he discovered a great lacuna as he went over his sources (1:1-2). These previous works were written by men and presented Jesus' ministry in a typical man's world. Women were hardly mentioned except at the close of Matthew and Mark, where specific names, Mary Magdalen and others, are provided three times as witnesses of the death, burial and resurrection of Jesus (e.g., Mark 15:40,47; 16:1). It almost looks as though they were reluctantly and somewhat embarrasingly mentioned because only women were the key witnesses of these central events. This was because all of Jesus' male disciples had left him and fled (Mark 14:50; Matt. 26:56).
     Modern scholarship[20] indicates that at least some of this

---

[20]For example, the very thorough study of Elisabeth Schüssler Fiorensa, *In Memory of Her: A Feminist Theological Reconstruction of Christian Origins* (N.Y., Crossroads, 1983) Also Winsome Monroe, "Women Disciples in Mark," *Catholic Biblical Quarterly* 44 (1982) 225-241

omission is deliberate in view of the patriarchal structures of
the gospel audiences in the ancient world. Luke however
read in between the lines, consulted special sources and
found that the great paradox of women in Jesus' ministry
was indeed present. If Luke read Mark 15:40-42, he would
surely have noticed that Mary Magdalene, Mary, Mother of
James and Joses as well as Salome were not recent disciples.
They were long-time followers of Jesus from Galilee and
had come up to Jerusalem along with *many other women*
(Mark 15:42).

Consequently, it became an important priority for Luke
to restore this place of women. Joel's prophecy had pointed
to an extraordinary paradox in the work of the Spirit
among women, young or old, free or slave in comparison to
a male dominated world. As an important step, Luke restored women to their rightful place in the entourage of
Jesus' disciples. Luke described Jesus' tour of cities and
villages of Galilee and then noted:

> The twelve were with him, and also some women
> who had been healed of evil spirits and infirmities:
> Mary called Magdalene from whom seven demons had
> gone out, and Joanna, the wife of Chuza, Herod's
> steward, and Susanna, and many others. (8:1-3)

This close association of Jesus with women was one more
unexpected surprise to the male-dominated religion of the
times. Teachers of that time simply did not accept women
disciples. In addition, Jewish men did not usually speak to
non-family women in public. The gospel of John notes that
Jesus' disciples were astonished at Jesus' speaking with a
woman (4:27). This was due to the fear of "catching" the
contagious legal uncleanness that women incurred for seven
days each month according Lev. 15:19-24. To this must be
added that some of the women, according to Luke's description, were cured of afflictions that would have made them
seem "unstable" to most people. Mary Magdalen had previously "seven devils" within her (8:2). This was perhaps a
way of saying that she was at least a lively character in her

day! Luke also notes that some of the women had considerable means at their disposal, for they provided for the support of Jesus and his companions (8:3). This also seems to imply that some of them had a great deal of independence.

All of this point to an unusual paradox in Jesus' ministry. His attitude toward women ws a striking contrast to many stern religious leaders of his time who shunned contact with women. Jesus must have smiled at this ridiculous contrast, but some people laughed at it in a different way, calling Jesus a friend of tax collector and sinners (7:34). The Baptist was accused of welcoming prostitutes, (Matt. 21:32) and no doubt some of Jesus' women disciples were labelled in the same way.

Luke makes every possible effort to present the unusual importance of women in the events of the New Age. He points out how extraordinary women took a special initiative in key events. For every Jew, Abraham was the father of all believers, the source of blessing for the nations (Gen. 12:3). In Luke's "protogospel" (chaps. 1 and 2), instead of Abraham, Mary is the mother and model of all believers: "Blessed is she who has believed that there would be a fulfilment of what as spoken to her from the Lord" (1:45). Luke carefully applies to Mary the expressions used of Abraham in the Old Testament. Abraham likewise was praised for his faith (Gen. 15:6). The same words, "Nothing is impossible with God" are addressed both to Abraham and Mary (Gen. 18:14; Luke 1:37). God tells Abraham that his wife Sarah will be blessed to become a mother of nations (Gen. 17:15-16). Elizabeth announces to Mary that she will be the most blessed among women (1:43).

Another extraordinary woman was Elizabeth the mother of the Baptist. Her husband Zechariah stalled and hesitated when the angel Gabriel announced that the aged couple would have a child (1:18). Not so, however, with Elizabeth. On the contrary she was a women of unusual insight. By movement of the Spirit (1:42) she recognized Mary as mother of the Messiah and gave her a special blessing. Like Sarah, the mother of Isaac, Elizabeth is a mother of joy, laughter and rejoicing; her neighbors rejoice with her that she is to become a mother in her old age. However, the family stops short of recongizing something more in the child. They prepare to circumcise the cild and name him after his father (1:59). At this point Elizabeth took the daring initiative to contradict all of them. Mindful of the angel's message, she said, "Not so; he shall be called John." Following the courageous breakthrough of faith on the part of Elizabeth, Zechariah finally came through, asking for a writing tablet and scribbling, "John is his name" (1:63).

Luke completes his picture of the paradox of women by being the only evangelist to record a number of stories and actions of other women: Anna the old prophetess came into the Temple to bless the child Jesus just at the very time he was presented in the Temple; the resurrection of the widow of Naim's son (7:11-17); the anointing of Jesus' feet by a penitent women (7:36-50); the visit of Jesus to the house of Martha and Mary (10:38-42); the woman in the crowd who blessed Jesus' mother (11:27-28); the cure of the stooped woman on the Sabbath (13:10-17); a parable about a woman and her lost coins (15:8-10); the widow and the unjust judge (18:1-8); the faithful daughters of Jerusalem who follow Jesus to the cross (23:27-31).

However, in all of this, the great question in the early church was whether women would express their faith by devotion to their traditional roles at home, or would they act as independent persons and disciples. Especially in the Jewish world, but also to a great extent in the Greek world, a woman's social and economic status was determined in relationship to men. As unmarried, she was under obedience to her father; as married, to her husband. Her principal role was to serve and nourish the men within the home. What then was to be the role of a woman disciple? Was her family role memely enhanced, or were new possibilities open to her? This must have been an important question in the early church. We have already observed the prominent role of women in the Acts of the Apostles. What they accomplished was not in their roles as mothers or wives but as independent persons and disciples. Yet this was not an age when careers for women were an option. Most Christian women would act out their lives and commitment to Christ within their homes. However, was there any precedent, a word from the Lord that might serve as guidance for Christian women in the New Way?

Luke seems to have brought in the story of Martha and Mary, found only in his gospel, to answer this important question. The story is simple, short and very much to the point. It begins as follows: "He (Jesus) entered a village; and a women named Martha received him into her house" (10:38). Already the story is unusual. Martha and Mary have their own home; husbands, father or children are not mentioned. It would indeed be exceptional for a great teacher and his male disciples to visit a strictly feminine household.

> And she had a sister called Mary, who sat at
> the Lord's feet and listened to his teaching. But
> Martha was distracted with much serving. (10:38-39)

Martha appears to be the older woman; she welcomes Jesus into the home and is responsible for the hospitality. The sight of at least a dozen hungry and thirsty disciples moved her quickly to the efficient action for which so many years of training had prepared her. Mary the younger seems oblivious to all this. She is seated at the Lord's feet. This is a technical expression for a disciple, as in 8:35 where the cured demoniac is "sitting at the feet of Jesus." We still use the expression "to sit at the feet of the master." The triple use of the name *Lord* strengthens this position. As a disciple, Mary listens to Jesus' teachings with a mind to obey them and put them into practice.

The busy and anxious Martha is overwhelmed with the needs of hospitality. She does not merely call Mary, but goes directly to Jesus and says, "Lord, do you not care that my sister has left me to serve alone? *Tell her then to help me*" (10:40). Note the repeated use of the title *Lord* and an appeal for a word or commandment of the Lord to solve the problem. In this way Luke skilfully has the story transcend the situation to answer the church's search for a word of the

Lord to answer their own questions.

> But the *Lord* answered, 'Martha, Martha, you
> are anxious and troubled about many things;
> one thing is needful. Mary has chosen the
> good portion, which shall not be taken away
> from her. (10:41-42)

We note that Martha is by no means condemned for her devoted traditional role of feminine hospitality. It is much needed and appreciated. However, the freedom of the younger sister to fully obey Jesus as a free and independent disciple has distinct priority over her obligation to obey her older sister and assist her in a traditional woman's role. This has great consequences for Luke's church. It sums up the theme of the paradox of women in Jesus' ministry. For Luke, the New Age can never really arrive until the prophecy of Joel is fulfilled concerning the restoration and full equality of women through the work of the Spirit.

8

The Sign of Jonah the Comic Prophet

Both Matthew (12:38-42; 16:1-4) and Luke give special attention to the strange sign of Jonah that will indicate the truth of Jesus' mission. Luke puts it this way:

> This generation is an evil generation,
> it seeks a sign, but no sign shall be
> given to it except the sign of Jonah.
> For as Jonah became a sign to the men
> of Nineveh, so will the Son of Man be
> to this generation. (11:29-30)....

The story of Jonah is the most humorous in the bible. He is a reluctant Hebrew prophet, literally forced to preach to Nineveh, capital of the Assyrians. These people were traditional enemies of the Jews. They had invaded Northern Israel and forced a large part of the population into exile. The background of the story, and the intentions of the author, must be understood to appreciate the humor of the story. The book was written after many Jews returned from the exile, probably during the 5th century B.C. or after.

Many of the returnees developed a very defensive and exclusive attitude toward the non-Jewish world. This is especially illustrated by the post-exilic books of Ezra and Nehemiah. Ezra the priest relates that the fervent returnees celebrated the Passover and separated themselves from the "pollutions of the peoples of the land to worship the LORD, the God of Israel" (6:21). He warned the people not to intermarry with any other peoples because of their abominations and pollution of the land (9:10-12). The priest even made the men pledge to dismiss wives who were foreigners, along with their children (10:1-4). Cf. Also Nehemiah 10:28,30-31.

The author of the book of Jonah tries to counteract these views by presenting God's views toward the Gentiles in comic contrast. The book opens with the words,

> Now the word of the LORD came to
> Jonah the Son of Amittai, saying,
> 'Arise, go to Nineveh, that great
> city, and cry against it; for their
> wickedness has come up before me.'

Jonah is thoroughly shocked. In all history, no Hebrew prophet has ever been sent to Gentiles, let alone their worst enemies the Babylonians. Hebrew prophets preached to their own people, usually to give them hope against threats of Gentiles and provide promises of eventual victory over them!

> But Jonah arose to flee to Tarshish
> from the presence of the LORD.
> he went down to Joppa and found a
> ship going to Tarshish; he paid
> the fare, and went on board, to
> go with them to Tarshish, away from
> the presence of the Lord. (1:2-3)

Jonah is such a provincial and narrow man that he thinks God is only the God of the Hebrew land, and that he can leave his presence by taking a ship for Spain (Tarshish, the end of the earth in those days). The Lord, however, is creator of heaven and earth and shows his universality by sending a mighty storm that threatened the little ship with destruction. The "pagan" mariners were afraid, and turned to prayer. They were astonished that Jonah was so irreligious that he slept in the hold at a time like this. The captain came to him and asked him to pray to his god. (1:7). As the storm grew worse and everyone's life was in danger, the sailors examined their consciences to see if any personal sins might be the cause of such a disaster. No one confessed, so they drew lots, which fell on Jonah. Jonah finally confessed his sin of disobedience to God, and asked to be thrown overboard. The sailors were very reluctant to do so. We notice the contrast between prayerful, sensitive Gentiles and the insensitive, irreligious Jonah. Finally, as a last resort he was thrown overboard, with the feeling that God wanted this punishment. However, God's purpose is not thwarted by this; he sends a large fish to swallow Jonah. In the belly of the "whale," the prophet has the beginnings of a conversion experience as he begins to pray to God. As a result the fish vomits him up on dry land.

A second command comes to Jonah, making God's intention all the more certain: "Arise, go to Nineveh, that great city, and proclaim to it the message that I tell you" (3:1). Then follow all kinds of surprises. Jonah is able to preach to a city so great that it takes three days' journey even to walk around it. Somehow he communicates to strangers with a different language. His preaching is so successful that there is universal repentance and change. Even the king "arose from his throne, removed his robe, and covered himself with sackcloth, and sat in ashes" (3:6). Jonah had preached, "Yet forty days and Nineveh shall be overthrown." The Babylonians, however, trusted in God's mercy to outweigh his anger so they would not be punished. As a result, "When God saw what they did, how they turned from their evil way, God repented of the evil which he had said he would do to them; and he did not do it" (3:10).

This was another great shock for Jonah. Here was a God who even changed his mind about the Gentiles! Jonah could now justify his flight to Tarshish and say, "That is why I made haste to flee to Tarshish; for I knew you were a gracious God and merciful, slow to anger, abounding in steadfast love, and repenting of evil" (4:2). Jonah was so disappointed that he wanted to die. He built a hut for himself outside the city where he could watch what might happen to it, still hoping it could be destroyed. The magic and comical details of the story continue as God makes a tree grow to give Jonah shade, and then causes it to wither. Jonah was so angry about this that he asked God to die. God contrasts Jonah's concern with himself, to the prophet's lack of concern about the lives of thousands of people in the city:

> You pity the plant, for which you
> did not labor, nor did you make it
> grow, which came into being in a
> night, and perished in a night, And
> should not I pity Nineveh, that
> great city, in which there are more
> than a hundred and twenty thousand
> persons who do not know their right
> hand from their left, and so much
> cattle? (4:10-11)

Luke's gospel was written to show that God's plan in the Scriptures has been fulfilled in surprising new ways. For Luke, God's most laughable surprise is the place and success of the Gentile mission in the divine plan. This was something completely unexpected, both by the Jews and by Jesus' own disciples. Most of the Scriptures did indeed have a place for the Gentiles, but it was always secondary and under Israel. For example, Isaiah saw them coming up to Jerusalem in the last days for instruction in a subservient position under the God of Isreal and his people (2:2). Zechariah pictured a great victory of Israel over the nations, with the survivors coming up to Jerusalem each year to worship at the feast of booths (14-16). Any nation that did not do so would be severely punished (14:17-18). Such nationalist pictures should of course be expected. Nation and religion always went together. The Lord guided Jewish history, and it was expected that a Jewish Messiah would first of all be for the Jewish people. To think of him favoring other nations would be as unbelievable as a statement that George Washington, our founder, was a Russian Messiah born in Moscow.

In addition to this, any significant association between Jews and Gentiles was almost a psychological, social and religious impossibility. The strict food and table fellowship laws of the Jews made it impossible for them to eat food prepared by Gentiles or to enter Gentile homes. Gentile and Jew lived in worlds apart. The whole system of Jewish and social education made it necessary to adopt a lifestyle with the close support of other fellow Jews in a definite city area, or to have a city of town of their own. This was true not only of Jews but Jewish Christians as well. The early converts frequented the Temple and synagogue, and kept all the requirments of the Law in regard to foods and table fellowship.

The sign of Jonah meant so much for Luke because he saw the comic Jonah come to life in early church. Jonah was so much like many Christian leaders who could not picture a Gentile apostolate so successful that Jewish Christians could even become a minority in many Christian communities. The early church at first pictured that the kingdom of God would be embodied in a renewed Jewish people, with the Gentiles added on. Luke has the early disciples asking the Risen Jesus, "Lord, will you at this time restore the kingdom to Israel?" (Acts 1:6). However, Jesus replies that this must wait until the Holy Spirit *first* makes them witnesses to Jerusalem, Judea, Samaria and even the ends of the earth (1:8). In his second volume, Luke points out how this was realized in such a surprising way by the Holy Spirit that even Peter and the Twelve were completely shocked and amazed.

The Acts of the Apostles makes it clear that it was not the twelve who initiated the unexpected world apostolate. Unnamed disciples from Cyprus and Cyrene in Africa brought the gospel to Antioch, where for the first time in world history there were Greek Christians and a mixed community of Gentiles and Jews (11:19-26). Acts centers about the work of Paul and his companions where the Gentile apostolate was so successful that they vastly outnumbered a small minority of Jewish converts (13:44-52;17:10-15;19:8-10).

In contrast, we see the humorous paradox of other Christian leaders who either were stunned by it all or even tried to stem the tide. Peter at first appears much like the reluctant Jonah in this regard. Peter's strict views on food laws and table fellowship are illustrated by the vision or revelation he received while in Joppa, the same seaport from which Jonah had left to try to flee from the Lord. In the vision, Peter saw a large canvas let down from the sky with all kinds of unclean animals on it. A voice told Peter to kill and eat their meat. Peter answered, "No Lord; for I have never eaten anything common or unclean." The voice then said, "What God has cleansed, you must not call common" (10:11-16). The vision was repeated three times, underlining the importance and certainty of the message. While Peter pondered over the message of the dream, some messengers came from Cornelius a Roman centurion at Caesarea, the Roman capital of the province they called Palestine. Peter, contrary to his custom, but mindful of his dream, accompanied them to the Gentile city and even into the centurion's house. Peter then said to him, "You yourselves know how unlawful it is for a Jew to associate with or to visit any one of another nation; but God has shown me that I should not call any man common or unclean"(10:28).

Like the book of Jonah that describes prayerful and responsive Gentiles in contrast to the prejudiced prophet, Cornelius is a remarkable contrast to Peter's stereotypes. Cornelius and his whole household is devout. He is very generous in his alms to the poor; he prays constantly to God (10:1-2). The question as to whether Peter and his Jewish companions can really associate together is solved not only by the triple voice in Peter's vision but even by the Holy Spirit, who comes down equally on the Gentiles as they listen to Peter's message. Luke describes them as praising God and speaking in tongues just as at the first Jewish Christian Pentecost (10:46; 2:4). Thus Peter feels obligated to baptize all the Gentiles without further obligations (10:47-48).

We can gauge something of the surprise of all this by the reaction of many Christians in Jerusalem when they heard about it. They said to Peter, "Why did you go to uncircumcised men and eat with them." (11:3)? Peter had to defend himself by explaining how he was justified to make this exception to the Law by a voice from heaven, and the coming of the Holy Spirit upon the joint assembly (11:1-18). Later on, when news of the great success of Paul and Barnabas with the Gentiles came to Jerusalem, there was so much criticism that it was necessary to call a meeting of the whole church, apostles and elders at Jerusalem to discuss the matter. The position of one group was phrased as follows: "Unless you (the Gentile converts) are circumcised according to the custom of Moses, you cannot be saved" (15:1). Their position was that the biblical laws were still in force. Jesus was after all a Jewish Messiah. A Gentile convert should first of all become a good Jew, and then believe in Jesus as the completion and fulfillment of the Law. Paul and his companions knew that in practice this would mean the end of the Gentile apostolate. Embracing circumcision, and all the precepts of the Law was like joining another nation and renouncing one's own. Likewise, it took away from the uniqueness and absolute power of the cross. This we know, not from Luke, but from Paul's letter to the Galatians (2:11-21). Paul's view finally prevailed, but at this conference a compromise in reference to foods was made so Jews would find table fellowship with Gentiles a workable possibility (Acts 15:6-29).

For Luke, it was only the Holy Spirit that made possible this remarkable turn in early Christianity. It enabled him to search the prophets for an alternate view of the place of the rest of the world in God's plan. Luke found the prophet Joel to be the best source. God had announced to Joel that there would be a great universal outpouring of the Spirit in the last times, with the final result that "Whoever calls on the name of the Lord shall be saved" (Acts 2:17-21; Joel 2:28-32). Because Luke had experienced this in his own life and experience, he was able to look for the same contrast in the life of Jesus, who became the sign of Jonah.

To avoid exclusivism, or any possible idea of a Jewish or Jewish Christian monopoly on the kingdom, Luke does not have Jesus, the Baptist or the twelve proclaim that the kingdom of God is *near*, as in the other gospels (Matthew 3:2; 4:17; 10:7; Mark 1:14). What is behind this? Luke wants his readers to realize that the coming kingdom is a world-wide phenomenon that does not takes place within the limited confines of Judaism or Jewish Christianity. To emphasize his point, Luke takes pains to show that Jesus actually counteracted the idea of the kingdom coming soon. In 19:11, Jesus relates the parable of the "talents" because some "supposed the kingdom of God was to appear imme-diately." In Luke's version of the parable, those who receive a special trust and use it well are given the reward of author-ity over "ten cities" or "five." This seems to bring out the picture of an extension of the kingdom during the time before the return of the master. This would fit into the picture of a great world apostolate, extending the kingdom beyond the Jewish nation.

Accordingly, throughout the gospel Luke presents the paradox of a universal kingdom in contrast to the narrower views held by both disciples and people. Just as the prophet Jonah was surprised by righteous Gentiles, so Luke presents a "bad" Roman centurion, as a model of virtue. He is so generous that he even built a synagogue for the Jewish people (7:5). Jesus marveled at his faith and told the crowd that he had never seen anything like it in Israel (7:9). A Samaritan "outcast" is presented as a model for understand-ing what it means to be a neighbor (11:36-37). Every good Jew imagined they would some day join their fathers Abra-ham, Isaac, Jacob and all the prophets in a great victory banquet over the Gentiles. However, Luke presents a rather comic picture of the great Jewish patriarchs having dinner with a host of "unwashed" Gentiles from the north, south, east and west (13:28-30). Those who felt they were the *included* ones and the Gentiles the *excluded* ones find the position reversed: "Behold some who are last who will be first, and some are first who will be last (7:30)."

Perhaps the most striking contrast in Luke is the mission of the 72, which is found nowhere else in the gospels. It is described in universal terms. The messengers are told to "eat what is set before them." This hints that the food obstacle to Gentile fellowship, so difficult even for Peter, is to be overcome, It is only here that Jesus tells these disciples to proclaim that the kingdom is *near* (10:9,11). The nearness of the kingdom is especially connected with the completion of the world apostolate. "The times of the Gentiles" must be completed (21:24). Only after this will the great universal return of the Son of Man take place, and people will know that "the kingdom of God is near (21:31)."

During the earthly life of Jesus, no such mission took place. In Matthew's gospel, Jesus forbade his disciples to go to the Gentiles or Samaritans (10:5). Mark sees it as something lying in the future. (13:10). What Luke has probably done, according to J. Fitzmyer[21], is to telescope directions given originally to the twelve with instructions given to apostles in the early church. Early Christian Apostles to the Gentiles claimed their authority from the Risen Lord. For example, Paul wrote, "Am I not an apostle? Have I not seen Jesus our Lord. (1 Cor 1:9)?" For Luke it is the one Lord, earthly and Risen who 'appointed' 72 others (10:1). It is also surprising that their number is six times greater than that of the twelve, whose mission was centered on the Jews. This hints that their harvest in the Gentile world far surpasses that of twelve. The importance of this for Luke is confirmed by the last words of Jesus in his gospel, which promise that repentance and forgiveness will be preached to all the nations. (24:47).

Luke would see the sign of the comic Jonah as one that must be perpetually renewed if the church is to be faithful to its mission. There are no outsiders, aliens and foreigners for

[21]In the Jerome Biblical Commentary, p. 143 (N.T. pagination)

someone who appreciates as Luke the oneness of the human family because we are all children of Adam and Eve (3:38). The laugher of Abraham at Isaac's birth echoes again at the final banquet of the kingdom of God as Abraham and Sarah laugh once more when they find themselves seated with all the unexpected children they were promised when God told them they would be fathers and mothers of many nations. (Genesis 12:2-4; 17:4,16).

9

Paradoxical Parables

Luke himself is a master storyteller. His special insight into comic eschatology enables him to find a special new dimension in the parables of Jesus. It also helps him introduce many original new stories found only in his gospel. Here we can only select a few that will illustrate Luke's sensitivity to the extreme paradox in Jesus' parables, a paradox the evangelist especially appreciates because he has seen it come alive in his own experience. We will begin with the parable of the sower. This is also found in Mark and Matthew. However, since it has so many Lucan "twists," it can serve to illustrate the author's fresh outlook on Jesus' teaching.

Luke's version of this parable is much shorter than that of Mark (4:1-9;13-20) and Matthew (13:1-9;18-23), because he wants to focus on the paradoxical elements and not get lost in detail.

> A sower went out to sow his seed
> and as he sowed, some fell along
> the path, and was trodden under
> foot and the birds of the air de-
> voured it. And some fell on the

> rock; and as it grew up, it with-
> ered away, because it had no
> moisture. And some fell among
> thorns and the thorns grew with
> it and choked it, and it yielded
> no grain. (8:5-7)

The audience of Jesus, and that of Luke were people close to the earth, and well acquainted with farming methods. Their first reaction would be that the farmer in the story was a fool. Why such a prodigious waster of seed? Any farmer knew well that throwing seed on a hard path only results in a feast for birds. Experience also teaches that sowing seed on rocky ground or thorns is a pure waste of seed, time and energy. It is only the second part of the parable that brings out the elements of complete contrast, gift, and surprise.

> And some fell into good soil and
> grew and yielded a hundredfold.
> (8:8)

If the parable ended with good seed, good soil and rich harvest, the end effect would be that of failure. An ordinary harvest yielded at the most an eight to tenfold yield. Such a result could hardly make up for the tremendous loss of all the seed that went on the paths, rocky ground and among thorns. But this yield is a *hundredfold*, an utterly amazing and impossible harvest that could only be brought about by divine action. Such a yield is described in the bible as due only to a powerful blessing of God, as in Genesis 26:12, "And Isaac sowed in that land and reaped in the same year a hundredfold. The Lord blessed him." Such a harvest, then, is the blessing of a true son of Abraham, like Isaac.

So the parable illustrates that God's action in the kingdom is a complete paradox. He is a foolish farmer, from a human standpoint, wasting his powerful seed where there will only be complete or partial failure. Yet this very contradiction shows who he is, and brings out the quality of grace: he prodigiously bestows his gifts where they are least expected and even least appreciated. Human views of the kingdom would expect him to select "good ground," but instead he selects "bad ground" for most of his work.

The parable, of course, illustrates the ministry of Jesus, as God's agent. He bestows special love even on Judas, although he knows the devil will snatch the seed out of his heart. Later Luke takes special note that "Satan entered into Judas called Iscariot who was one of the number of the twelve" (22:3). Jesus too had trouble with rocky ground: people who received him with enthusiasm but without real roots to continue on. It is interesting that Luke slightly changes the wording here. While Matthew and Mark have "rocky ground," Luke has simply "rock." Could this be an allusion to Peter (rock) who fell away in time of temptation? This hint is strengthened by the interpretation of the parable in 8:13, where it is applied to those who fall away in time of temptation. Only Luke has "temptation" instead of "tribulation and persecution" on the part of Matthew 13:21 and Mark 4:17. Luke emphasizes this temptation for Peter at the Last Supper (22:31) and twice in the agony in the garden (22:40,46). The seed among thorn could well apply to Jesus' call of a wealthy man who went away sad because he was very rich (18:23). Riches are explicitly mentioned in the interpreted parable in 8:14.

Luke treasures this parable because he has witnessed the Holy Spirit continuing the mission of Jesus through preachers of the word in the early church. In Luke's version of the interpreted parable, "The seed is the word of God (8:12)." This word offers the opportunity to "believe and be saved" (8:12). Luke understands the paradox because he has seen it in action. The Word of God goes everywhere as in the parable. It is a story of tremendous waste and apparent failure. Luke illustrates this in his Acts of the Apostles. Even at the daily distribution of bread for the hungry by the Jerusalem Christians, there is complaining and criticism (6:1-6). Paul has a bitter separation from Mark and Barnabas, his fellow apostles and companions (15:36-39). At Samaria, a certain Simon played a key role in the first opening of the gospel to the non-Jewish world. Yet he was tempted to offer money to Peter and Paul to obtain special powers (8:9-20). Two prominent early Jerusalem Christians, Ananias and Sapphira, sold property to help the poor but fell to the temptation of Satan (5:3) to deceive the apostles about the sum of the money.

Yet despite all this waste, the hundredfold harvest takes place as a remnant of people with good hearts everywhere accept the gospel. Luke makes special mention of the heart in the parable (8:12,15) and throughout the Acts of the Apostles (some 21 times). His conclusion of the seed parable interpretation sums things up:

> And as for that in the good soil,
> they are those who hearing the
> word, hold it fast in an honest
> and good heart and bring forth
> fruit with patience. (8:15)

This "patience" is mentioned only here and in 21:19. It is very important for Luke. Only a person who has the patience to experience failure in seeing good seed wasted can also experience the paradox of the hundredfold harvest.

A fitting companion to the above parable is that of the mustard seed, the "tiniest of all seeds on earth" according to Matthew 13:32 and Mark 4:31. Again, Luke does not wish to devote attention to details but to the central paradox.

> It is like a grain of mustard seed
> which a man took and sowed in his
> garden; and it grew and became a
> tree, and the birds of the air made
> nests in its branches. (3:19)

The theme is that of enormous hidden power within a hardly visible appearance. This is in direct contrast to the tremendous human energy expenditure on the part of so many religious leaders and their followers who felt they could "force" the coming of the kingdom by their efforts. In contrast, the parable pictures a minimum of effort. Modern readers with no experience of mustard seeds need another image, perhaps that of the unbelievable powers locked within the atom, that only need a relatively insignificant trigger to be released. The image of the mustard seed is found again in connection with faith. The apostles said to the Lord,

> Increase our faith! And the Lord
> said, 'If you had faith as a grain
> of mustard seed, you could say to
> this sycamore tree, 'Be rooted
> up, and be planted in the see
> and it would obey you.' (17:5-6)

The parable of the woman and the yeast illustrates further the same theme of hidden transforming power within very ordinary circumstances.

> And again he said, "To what shall
> I compare the kingdom of God? It
> is like leaven which a woman took
> and hid in three measures of flour,
> till it was all leavened. (13:20-21)

Luke has this parable in the context of Jesus' argument with the "wise and learned" ruler of a Synagogue concerning healing on the Sabbath. At the end of the encounter, Luke writes, "All his adversaries were put to shame; and all the people rejoiced at the glorious things done by him" (13:17). The parable coming at this point hints that the most uneducated peasant woman knows more about the action of the kingdom than Jesus' learned opponents. She knows that all she has to do is to "hide" a little bit of yeast in three measures of flour, and then do nothing for several hours. The mysterious inner power of the leaven will transform all the dough so that over a hundred loaves of bread can be baked.

We turn our attention now to parables found only in Luke. Best known among these is the "Good Samaritan." This parable has given rise to a host of Good Samaritan hospitals, and even a dictionary meaning: "A person who is compassionate and helpful to one in distress." (From The American Collegiate Dictionary) Dominic Crossan[22] has reminded us that to understand this parable we must put aside all these modern meanings. For Jesus' audience, the Samaritan was not "good" at all, nor were the priests and levites "bad." Just the opposite was true. Originally, the whole parable illustrated a comic paradox in which the good become bad and the bad become good.

The parable's setting is a question addressed to Jesus by a teacher of the Law, who asked, "Who is my neighbor?" (10:25). The question was asked after Jesus had reaffirmed that to love God and one's neighbor was sufficient to obtain eternal life. The story tells of a man who went along the treacherous road from Jerusalem to Jericho and was way-laid by robbers. They stripped him of everything he had, beat him up and left him lying half-dead by the side of the road. If we put aside our modern stereotypes, the people who came along were good and holy. They were a priest and Levite on the way to Jericho, which was a priestly city. Perhaps they were returning from Jerusalem after performing their sacred Temple ministry, or on the way to perform some sacred function in Jericho. They were good men anxious to fulfill the law in every detail of their lives. At a glance, the priest noticed the man lying by the wayside. He looked as though he was dead. As a priest he was supposed to guard his legal "cleanness" without which he could not perform his sacred functions for his people. Touching a dead body would make him unclean. This was no light matter. Priests were supposed to take every care to avoid "uncleanness" that would disqualify them from being of service to God and the people. In addition to this, purification was a long and costly process. The law prescribed a ceremonial bath with a special holy water sprinkled with ashes of a red heifer. The expenses might mean a financial disaster to the family. With his mind churning over these legal requirements, the priest did not want to take any

[22] *Raids on the Articulate*, pp. 102-4

chances: "When he saw him he passed by on the other side" (10:31). In his fear he did not even want to come near, hence the observation that he went to the opposite side of the road. The same notation is made of the Levite, thus strengthening the story, for the Levite would have the same reasons.

Then the "enemy" and "bad person" comes along. The Samaritan was regarded as an enemy and foreigner. Actually, they were half Jews ethnically, but because they had intermarried with foreigners at the time of the exile, the returnees refused to accept them. They were not allowed to enter the Temple, and consequently built their own sacrificial place of worship. There were numerous conflicts between Jews and Samaritans. It was very often unsafe for a Jew to travel through their territory.

The "bad person" does what is completely unexpected of him. Not troubled with a brain whirling with religious regulations, he simply lets himself be moved by the situation and acts accordingly. Letting himself be moved by his compassionate heart rather than by his head, the "enemy" acts in a "foolish" manner, in contrast with "wise" and calculating approach of the two previous good men. He not only provides needed emergency treatment, but puts aside all other tasks to spend time with the helpless man. Pressed to leave for home, he entrusts the battered victim to the innkeeper, leaving a considerable sum for future care and promising to give more on his return if necessary.

Jesus then asks the Law teacher which of the people showed himself as neighbor to the victim of robbery and mugging. The lawyer carefully avoids saying "the Samaritan," but makes it almost anonymous by saying, "The one who showed mercy on him." Jesus answered, "Go and do likewise" (10:37). For a modern audience to appreciate the paradox, we would have to picture something like a minister, priest or nun as obviously good people absorbed in their religious duties but passing by on the other side. In contrast we would have to imagine someone like an atheistic Marxist or pimp with no religious considerations on their minds, just letting their hearts be moved and responding appropriately. We would then appreciate the comic reversal and understand the paradox of the parable: the good become the bad and the bad become the good.

A similar parable of dramatic contrast is that of the Tax Collector and Pharisee in Luke 18:9-14. Once again, we are impeded from appreciating the comic reversal by our stereotypes of "Pharisee." This stereotype has found its way into the English language with the word "pharisaical," meaning, "a righteous or hypocritical person." (From the *American College Dictionary*) In Jesus' time and in Luke's, later on, a Pharisee was a person who embodied everything that was good in their zeal for perfect observance of the law in even the most minute matters. As respected and popular teachers, they were the cream of Judaism.

> Two men went up to the temple to
> pray, one a pharisee and the other
> a tax collector. The Pharisee
> stood and prayed thus with himself,
> 'God, I thank thee that I am not
> like other men, extortioners, un-
> just, adulterers, or even like this
> tax collector.' (18:10-11)

In complete contrast, the tax collector represents the worst possible kind of a person: a betrayer of his own people through a livelihood characterized by injustice and service of foreign Roman oppressors. There is nothing wrong with the Pharisee's prayer; he is a good man, and thanks God for the ability to be different from ordinary sinners. He stands up to pray in the custom of the times. His great devotion to God is shown by his fasts each week (accompanied by prayer) and by giving tithes on everything (18:12). In the ordinary interpretation, tithes on grain, wine and oil fulfilled the law, but the Pharisee wanted to make his service of God as complete and total as possible.

> But the tax collector, standing
> far off, would not even lift up
> his eyes to heaven, but beat his

breast saying, 'God be merciful
to me a sinner!' I tell you,
this man went down to his house
justified more than the other.
(18:13-14)

The ending is unexpected. God's ways and standards are simply not our ways. D. Crossan[23] sums this up well as follows:

> The literal point of the parable
> is a startling story of situa-
> tional reversal in which the
> virtuous Pharisee is rejected by
> God and the sinful publican gains
> approval. The metaphorical chal-
> lenge is again clear: the complete,
> radical, polar reversal of accepted
> human judgment, even or especially
> of religious judgment, whereby the
> Kingdom forces its way into human
> awareness. What, in other words,
> if God does not play the game
> by our rules?

[23]*In Parables,* p. 69

10

Spectacular Parties for the Hungry

This title is not an exaggeration, but really an understatement of an economic miracle and paradox in Luke that even today makes many people laugh either in disbelief or complete surprise. Miracles of healing are one matter, for most people recognize that there are mysterious inner powers of human nature that are not understood. External and economic miracles are often a much greater challenge. Once again, Luke writes about these things because he has actually seen them happen. In the Acts of the Apostles, he describes a special daily free meal for the poor and hungry that was provided by generous Jerusalem Christians (6:1-3). It was so important for them that the Twelve themselves personally administered it, until the numbers grew so large that they had to look for assistants (6:2).

Luke sums up the paradox of this chapter through part of the song of Mary when she visits Elizabeth: "he (God) has filled the hungry with good things, and the rich he has sent empty away" (1:53). The same contrast is announced in the beatitudes. Jesus pronounces a special blessing upon the hungry: "Blessed are you that hunger now, for you shall be satisfied" (6:20). In contrast the selfishness of those who are full and rich brings a curse upon them: "Woe to you that are full now, for you shall hunger" (6:25). Luke is quite conscious of the comic contrast in these matters, as he writes Jesus' words: "Blessed are you that weep now, for you shall laugh," and "Woe to you that weep now, for you shall laugh," and "Woe to you that laugh now, for you shall mourn and weep." (6:21, 25). Right from the beginning of his gospel Luke is concerned, almost obsessed, with the question of food.[24] Only in his gospel do we find the practical response of John the Baptist to the multitudes who come to his baptism and ask for practical advice in the words, "What then are we to do?" (3:10). The Baptist responds very simply and concretely:

> He who has two cloaks, let him share with him who has none; and he who has food, let him do likewise. (3:11)

Luke is anxious to present Jesus as a model in this whole question of food for the hungry. The evangelist does this especially through the story of the Multiplication of the Loaves, which he sees not as a spectacular event of the past but as a continuing miracle in his church. In explaining this miracle, Luke almost certainly has in mind the spiritual food of the Eucharist, since the wording of the distribution of bread is similar to that of the last supper (9:16; 22:19). However, the basic action is a simple sharing of food[25] among hungry people, and Luke could not separate this from the spiritual food of the Eucharist. The miracle of the loaves is highlighted not only in Luke but in all the gospels. It marks the climax of a series of Jesus miracles, and comes just before Peter's confession of faith. It has this central

[24]The prominent place of food in Luke's gospel is given special attention in my book; cf. note 18 above.

[25]Monika Hellwig makes a point of this in her book, *The Eucharist and the Hunger of the World* (N.Y., Paulist Press, 1976) p. 10

place because it is meant to parallel[26] and even surpass the greatest epiphanies of God in Jewish history: the miraculous manna and the Red Sea crossing.

Accordingly, we must first turn to the Old Testament story to receive the full impact of Luke's message. The setting is the barren peninsula of Sinai, where the Israelites have depleted their food supplies and are unable to obtain or buy more provisions. In desperation, the people cry out to Moses, their leader, and to God for help. God answered their prayer and said, "In the morning you shall be filled with bread: then you shall know that I am the Lord your God" (Ex. 16:12). Accordingly, when the people arose in the morning, they found, "A fine flake-like thing, fine as hoar frost on the ground." (Ex. 16:15). So they exclaimed in Hebrew, "Man hu?," (root of the word *manna*) meaning, "what is this?" Moses answered, "It is the bread which the LORD has given you to eat." God then commanded them, "Gather of it, every person among you, as much as he/she can eat."

In addition to the primary miracle of God's provision of food for the hungry, there is also a secondary but very important element in the story. There was sufficient bread for everyone only beause a second miracle of sharing also took place. In the story, every able-bodied person went out to gather the miraculous food. There were, of course, many sick, elderly and disabled people who could not do this. Even among those who did go out, some were able to gather much larger amounts than others. Yet God commanded that all should share the food equally at the end of the day, regardless of the amount they gathered. In this way, the old, the sick, the handicapped, the weak and feeble all shared equally in receiving provisions. The Israelites obeyed God's command, and the bible notes that when they measured out the bread, "he that gathered much had nothing over, and he that gathered little had no lack" (16:18). Accordingly, eve-

---

[26]The epiphanic nature of this and other miracles as parallel to the O.T. is brought out by Paul Achtemeir, "The Origin and Function of the Pre-Markin Miracle Catenae," *Journal of Biblical Literature* 91 (1972) pp. 198-221

ryone had enough to eat. It is often overlooked that this "miracle of sharing" also has an important place in the Multiplication of Loaves.

The New Testament loaves story, in striking parallel to the Exodus account, still retains the primary elements of a miraculous sharing of good. The crowds in the gospel story, like those of Exodus, are in a desperate situation. Both groups are in a desert place far from their homes and any supply of food. The disciples express the need to Jesus, just as the Israelites went to Moses. Jesus replied by way of an impossible command, "You yourselves give them to eat" (9:13). All the gospels record the sense of frustration at the impossible nature of Jesus' command. In Mark's gospel, the meaning becomes more implicit as Jesus adds, "How many loaves have you? Go and see" (8:18). These words direct the disciples to search and find out if there are any people who have bread they are willing to share. The disciples find only five or seven loaves in the various accounts, and this seems a ridiculously small amount for a huge crowd. John's gospel highlights this matter for laughter by having a child come up to the disciples with a few loaves and dried fish he had been saving as a picnic lunch for traveling (6:9). Yet it was done in answer to Jesus' impossible command, and that is the important matter. Without this first sharing, Jesus' further action could not have taken place. In other words, a miracle of sharing helps to initiate the loaves miracle. It is an obedient response to Jesus' command, "You yourselves give them to eat." In Jesus' command, the addition (though not needed) of the Greek second person pronoun adds special emphasis to the command given the disciples: *You yourselves* are the ones who should provide the food.

We have emphasized the command aspect because we will see signs that Luke considers Jesus' impossible command and laughing paradox as continuing[27] to be addressed to the church. First, however, let us present another indication of

---

[27]The following article attempts to illustrate Jesus' command as a continual address to the church: J. Grassi, "You Yourselves Give Them To Eat," *Bible Today* (1978) pp. 1704-1709

the centrality of the command feature. The Old Testament has first of all shown that it was God's command that enabled the starving Israelites to find bread to eat in the Sinai desert. In addition, the gospels' loaves miracle forms a literary parallel to a similar loaves miracle by the prophet Elisha in 2 Kings 4:42-44,

> A man came from Baal shalishah, bringing the man of God bread of the first fruits, twenty loaves of barley, and fresh ears of grain in his sack. And Elisha said, 'Give to the men, that they may eat.' But his servant said, 'How am I to set this before a hundred men?' So he repeated, 'Give them to the men, that they may eat, for thus says the Lord, "They shall eat and have some left." So he set it before them. And they ate, and had some left, according to the word of the Lord.

In this story the command of the prophet accomplishes its purpose because it has all the power of God behind it. The same is true of Jesus' words as a prophetic command which the church is to obey. We can note the parallels of this story to the gospels. (1) The order to give the people food; (2) the objections about the impossible command, and (3) the emphasis on the superabundant food and the leftovers.

We can now add some additional links between Jesus' distribution of bread for the hungry and that in the early church. Luke more than any other gospel gives special attention to bread and food. His version of the Lord's Prayer petition for bread reads, "Give us *each day* our daily bread" (11:3). Why does Luke add "each day" in comparison to Matthew (6:11)? It seems no accident that Luke uses the exact Greek words, *kath hēmeran* (each day or daily) to describe the continual distribution of bread to the hungry and poor in the early church (Acts 6:1). It is called the "daily distribution." Other connections are the following. In Luke's gospel, it is the *Twelve* who come to Jesus to ask him to dismiss the crowds so they can seek food and shelter (9:13). Jesus' command to provide food is addressed in the same verse to the Twelve. It is also the Twelve who direct the crowd to recline on the ground. Luke makes a point of their exact obedience to Jesus: "And they did so, and made them all sit down" (9:15). Likewise, it is the Twelve who preside over food distribution in the early community (Acts 6:1-3).

As in the miracle of the loaves, it is voluntary sharing that enables the miracle to start to take place. In the Acts of the Apostles, the daily meal for the hungry is made possible by Christians who are willing to make great sacrifices, even to the extent of selling houses and property so no one will remain hungry (Acts 3:44; 4:35). Once again, the Twelve have an important place (as in the loaves account) when they receive the donations from community members (4:35, 37; 5:1). In these texts, the gifts are laid "at the apostles' feet." The concern for the hungry was not just for local needs but for other communities as well. For example, the Antioch Christians responded to a famine by setting aside money and supplies for Christians living in Judea (11:27-30). This is in marked contrast to Herod the king in the next chapter, who is insensitive to his subjects' need for food (12:25).

It is interesting to note that the apostles' concern was not only for food but for other needs such as hospitality and lodging. Only in Luke, the Twelve in the loaves account are concerned that the crowds have no place to go to find shelter as well as provisions (9:12). We should also add the description in chapter 5 concerning Luke's banquet theme under the title "Feasts for Fools." The banquets of the kingdom of heaven are designed for the poor, the hungry, the sick, the handicapped, the outcasts, and the disadvantaged.

We can sum up as follows: Jesus' impossible command to his disciples to feed the hungry multitudes makes possible a comic contrast when it is listened to and obeyed. It fulfills the words of Mary, "he has filled the hungry with good things, and the rich he has sent empty away" (1:53). The hungry find they have the blessing of God promised by the Beatitudes (6:25) because they now share and "own" the food and property of every believer. The rich find themselves limited and "poor" in their own selfish possessions.

11

The Kingdom Is Child's Play

In many ways, children have always been the best teachers we have. Adults often get into such ruts and stereotypes that they no longer see things and people as they really are. They have so many past experiences and such future expectations that they are often no longer open to fresh insights from the here and now. A young child is usually able to become engrossed in the present moment and feel the beauty and wonder that it contains. Children become our teachers when they reopen the posibility of fresh new experience. They do this through their recovery of joy and meaning in ordinary things that have lost their meaning, or become routine for adults.

Luke gives more attention to children and childhood than any other gospel because they are the model for the openness to understanding the humorous paradoxes that teach the nature of the kingdom. The first passage to be discussed is the blessing of children (Luke 18:15-17; Mark 10:13-16; Matthew 19:13-15).

> Now they were bringing even infants to him that he might
> touch them; and when the disciples saw it they rebuked
> them. But Jesus called them to him, saying, 'Let the
> children come to me and do not hinder them; for to such
> belongs the kingdom of God. Truly, I say to you, whoever
> does not receive the kingdom of God like a child shall not
> enter it.' (18:15-17)

Luke omits some details found in Mark to heighten the
contrast. On one side, the busy and efficient disciples are
concerned that the Master's time be spent in winning over
the older and more influential people, especially leaders.
These latter were often called the "elders," because their age,
experience and power gave them a special position of
authority. In direct opposite, Jesus rebukes the disciples and
invites the little children to come to him. Then he says that
the kingdom of God belongs to them and that everyone
must become like a child to receive it. The paradox is
heightened by Luke when he uses the word "infants" at the
beginning of the story rather than "child." The infant is the
most powerless member of human society, the most suscept-
ible to harm as well as good. Yet it is the strongest in its
remarkable ability to be open to new experiences. Luke will
use the same word "infant," *brephos* in Greek, of the child
Jesus (1:41, 44; 2:12, 16).

A second text on children appears in an important context after the second prediction of Jesus' cross and death
(Mark 9:30-32; Luke 9:43-45). Matthew omits the story in
this contest, but some of the sayings are found in 18:1-5 and
20:26-27.

> And an argument arose among them as to which of them
> was the greatest. But when Jesus perceived the thought of
> their hearts he took a child and put him by his side, and
> said to them 'Whoever receives this child in my name
> receives me, and whoever receives me receives him who
> sent me; for he who is least among you all is the one who is
> great. (9:46-48)

The story is very similar to that in Mark 9:33-7, but once again Luke omits details and simplifies to emphasize the paradox. The word of the cross preceding the story is a key to its meaning. Jesus had explained to his disciples that he would be handed over to death by a betrayer, but they could not understand this saying, and were afraid to ask him. The word or the cross is the extreme example of weakness and lack of power. The disciples cannot accept it, and talk about the powerful coming of the kingdom and their places of authority within it. In Luke's version Jesus places the child at his side, the very place of authority that his disciples were arguing about! A child reigns with him. To receive this child is to receive the king at his side. Luke ends the story with the paradox that sums its meaning: "For he who is least among you all is the one who is great." (9:48). It will receive an even greater emphasis at the Last Supper when Jesus contrasts earthly rulers such as kings with leaders in the church: "Not so with you; rather let the greatest among you become as the youngest and the leader as one who serves" (22:26).

The Triumph of a Child: Luke's Christmas Story

Luke's Christmas story has become one of the best-known stories of the world. In some ways, this is an impediment rather than an advantage. The story is usually told as a beautiful factual event from the past, another monument of ancient history. When this happens, Luke's most masterful paradox providing the tone for his whole gospel becomes lost. Perhaps children's eyes are still most capable of understanding it: they are still able to gaze with wonder at a Christmas manger and become indentified with the scene that is presented to them. In this way they actually fulfill the teaching purpose of the Evangelist.

The secret of the Christmas story lies in the Old Testament Scriptures that Luke has carefully woven together in order to present the greatest living paradox of history. Central to the story is the sign of the manger, which is repeated three times in the story. First of all it is related that

Mary gave birth to her first-born son, wrapped him in swaddling clothes, "and laid him in a manger, because there was no place for them in the inn" (2:7). Secondly, an angel tells the shepherds that there will be a special sign by which they can recognize the birth of a Savior, who is Christ the Lord" (2:11). The angel says, "You will find a babe wrapped in swaddling clothes and lying in a manger." (2:12). Thirdly, the shepherds go over to Bethlehem to see what the Lord has made known to them. They find the child lying in a manger and understand what had been told about the child. (2:16).

What is the key of the shepherds' understanding that Luke wants his audience to grasp? The manger itself is very ordinary. It is a simply constructed bin of grain where domestic animals such as the ox, the donkey, or sheep can eat grain. It is essentially a place of eating and nourishment. To see its meaning in the story we must go back to the Old Testament Scriptures. Luke provides enough leads to direct us where to look. The central event is the long-awaited birth of a king, the son of *David*, as announced to Mary. (1:32). The child will also be the Son of God, through the special work of the Spirit (1:35). Key words in the story are first, *Bethlehem, City of David* (2:4; with the note that Joseph was of the house and lineage of David); also, (2:11, 15). It is especially noted that it was *while they were there* (2:6) the child was born. Then the title, *Christ, the Lord* (2:11), and the central place of *shepherds* in the story (2:8, 15, 18).

The function of such a king is central to Luke's meaning. The essential role of a king is one who shepherds or feeds (same word) his people. God said to David, Israel's first king, "You shall feed my people Israel" (2 Sam 5:2). Behind the king and working through him is God, who is the supreme shepherd, the one who feeds his people. Isaiah describes God 's coming to his people in these terms, "He will feed his flock like a shepherd, he will gather the lambs in his arms, he will carry them in his bosom, and gently lead those that are with young" (40:11). A favorite psalm for prayer based on this feeding and shepherding action began with the words, "The Lord is my shepherd, I shall not want: he makes me lie down in green pastures" (23:1).

In the hopes for a great future messianic age, prominent texts were those describing God as a shepherd feeding his people either directly or through a future king. Through the prophet Ezekiel, God contrasts himself with human shepherds who are concerned more for themselves — for wool and food — than for their sheep. In regard to the future king, God says, "I will set up over them, one shepherd, my servant David, and he shall feed them: he shall feed them and be their shepherd" (34:23). In regard to himself, God says,

> I myself will be the shepherd of my sheep, and I will make them lie down....I will seek the lost, and I will bring back the strayed....I will feed them in justice. (34:15-16)

With this scriptural backdrop we can now go to Luke 's story of the birth of Jesus. If we read it carefully, we will find that he has many close parallels to the narrative of the choice of David, Israel's first king. It will help to place them in parallel columns for easier study.

God said to Samuel the prophet; I will send you to Jesse the Bethlehemite, for I have provided for myself a king among his sons..... You shall anoint for me him whom I name to you" (2 Sam. 16:2-3).

Jesse is the father of David, mentioned in Luke 1:32:2:4,11,15; Bethlehem, 2:4,6. The anointing is to make him the king or anointed of the Lord, the *Christos* (2:12). The one chosen will be through God's own work, parallel to the sign of the manger by which the shepherds will be able to recognize who the child is (2:13).

Samuel did what the Lord commanded, and came to Bethlehem. The elders of

the city came to meet him;
trembling and said, "do you
come peaceably?" And he said,
"Peaceably" (16:2).

To bring peace on earth is
the mission of the messianic
king. (2:5).

Jesse, David's father, has
seven sons who impress Samuel
by their height and appearance. However, God tells the
prophet that none of these is
the one chosen. Samuel asks
if there are any others. And
the father replied, "there
remains yet the youngest
(literally, the little one)
but behold, he is keeping the
sheep" (16:11). With these
words, the prophet sent
for him (David) and anointed
him king over Israel (16:12-13).

The true king is not found
among the mighty and strong
but in a rustic setting
among shepherds, who are
mentioned in 2:8, 15, 18.

We are now prepared to find the sign of the manger that
Luke is so concerned about. We note that it is only simple
and humble shepherds who are able to find it. Shepherds are
people whose whole life is concerned with feeding. They
must know where to go to find nourishment for themselves
and their flocks. Children, and the youngest of the family,
like David, were often selected for this work, since they were
not fit for other tasks. In the story of Jesus' birth, shepherds
first receive the good news of the birth of the Messiah. To
them is revealed the sign of the manger which will lead them
to recognize him. They come to Bethlehem and find the
child lying in a manger with Mary and Joseph close by.
Then they recognize him. How did they do so? They knew
that the Lord was indeed the Shepherd of his people and
that he would send a king, who would feed his people like a

shepherd. Here was a child lying in a feeding trough, the very place they often fed their sheep and other animals. This extraordinary sight led them to a remarkable concurrence: this child was indeed the nourishment of this people! Children, and childlike shepherds would be open to this truth, a truth hidden from wise and learned scholars.

Another remarkable concurrence from the Scriptures would also lead them to recognize the child.[28] The first words of the greatest Old Testament prophet, Isaiah, had a mysterious mention of a manger:

> Sons have I reared and brought up,
> but they have rebelled against me.
> The ox knows its owner, and the
> ass its master's crib: but Israel
> does not know, my people do not
> understand. (1:2-3)

Isaiah is saying that the ass, traditionally the dumbest of animals, always knows where to go for its food. It goes to the crib (manger) of its owner (lord). However, people do not know that God (the lord) is the source of their nourishment. The sign of the manger in Luke is meant to be a challenge for the reader to understand the greatest paradox in human history: that a child, born in the simplest of surroundings and found by humble and childlike shepherds, could indeed be the promised shepherd and source of nourishment for his people. It is understood only in the realm of deepest faith.

There is also another element in the story that Luke may be using to heighten the great paradox of faith. In connection with the sign of the manger, Luke twice mentions that the child will be found wrapped in swaddling clothes. Why does he mention this detail? It is not a distinguishing mark, since the custom in those days was to wrap all babies in bands of cloth to keep their spines

[28]These background Scriptures for Luke's Christmans story are explained by Charles Giblin in his article, "Reflections on the Sign of the Manger," *Catholic Biblical Quarterly* 29 (1967) pp. 87-101

straight. As noted, Luke is concerned with the meaning of events as illustrated through the Scriptures. There is only one mention in the bible of swaddling clothes in connection with a king. This is in the book of Wisdom. The author in the name of Solomon states that he was born like any ordinary child in his mother's womb, carried there for ten months, cried when he was born, and was wrapped with *swaddling clothes*, for no *king* has any different kind of birth (7:4-5).

What then is the difference between him and any other king? It is the divine gift of wisdom: "I prayed and the spirit of Wisdom came to me" (7:7). Luke gives special attention to wisdom in his first two chapters. He mentions twice that the child Jesus grew in wisdom and God's grace (2:39, 52). Gradually, in the rest of the gospel, Luke will bring out that Jesus is the wisdom of God. The emphasis on swaddling clothes as part of the sign of the manger may be another way to present the challenging paradox that the most ordinary child in appearance may be recognized in faith not only as the messianic shepherd king, but even as the very Wisdom of God.

12

Humor in Prayer, or Answer Before You Ask

In human affairs, when we want something from some-one we usually ask them for it and then wait to see what the answer will be. In the Old Testament, prayers were made with great confidence based on God's presence in his people through his covenant. At the same time there were hesitations. Many biblical prayers contained constant reminders to God of his covenant or past favors. In constrast, Luke presents an unusual type of prayer based on the belief that the answer is already found in the question or address.

Luke's background for teaching prayer is the prayer of Jesus' himself: "He was praying in a certain place, and when he ceased, one of his disciples said to him, 'Lord, teach us to pray, as John taught his disciples' (11:1). In Luke's rendition of the Lord's Prayer, Jesus' address to God is contained in only one word, "Father." What follows this are the actual petitions or requests. Following the Lord's Prayer, Jesus in Luke illustrates this through the humorous parable of the friend requesting three loaves at midnight (11:5-13). This friend had an urgent request: another friend, famished from hunger, had come to his home from a journey. The laws of hospitality were an urgent priority in the ancient world. The host must take even extraordinary means to provide food and lodging for guests. Since he has nothing in the house, he goes to his friend even at midnight and knocks loudly at the door, shouting out his need in the street outside. The answer from within comes, "The door is shut, and my children are with me in bed; I cannot get up and give you anything" (11:7).

The request is actually much more difficult than the modern reader would imagine. In those days, no bread was kept from day to day. It was always freshly made each morning. To provide the requested loaves, the whole household would have to be aroused. A fire in the oven must be rekindled. The women would have to begin the long laborious task of grinding wheat, then making it into dough and finally baking the loaves. At least several hours would be involved. It is out of the question to begin all this at midnight even for a friend, and any reader will identify with the problem and agree. However, the importunate friend keeps pounding at the door and will not take "no" for an answer. No one in the house can sleep, and it looks as though the man will keep pounding and shouting indefinitely. And so the parable concludes: "I tell you, though he will not get up and give anything because he is his friend, yet because of his importunity he will rise and give him whatever he needs" (11:8). And again the reader will agree; it is the only thing to do. There are few human beings who will not give in, if only to get peace and quiet. In other words, it is hard to refuse a determined, persevering request. If this is so with human beings, is it not preeminently so about God, the *Father*, the friend of friends? The answer is so sure, that all you have to do is keep asking to show your confidence and persistence.

With this prelude, Luke attaches a teaching of Jesus on prayer found elsewhere in Matthew in the Sermon on the Mount.

> Ask and it will be given you;
> seek, and you will find;
> knock and it will be opened

> to you. For everyone who asks
> receives, and he who seeks finds,
> and to him who knocks it will
> be opened. (7:7-8)

Even Jesus' saying has a persistent note to it. The present tense of the verb is used in each case: "keep on asking; keep on seeking; keep on knocking." Three different images are used to bring out the persevering theme, and then the whole thing is repeated in another form to provide the greatest possible certainty: "For everyone who asks, receives. . . . . etc." The basis for this certainty goes back to the prayer of Jesus, "Father" which is now applied to the believer:

> What father among you, if his son
> asks for a fish, will instead of
> a fish give him a serpent; or if
> he asks for an egg, will give him
> a scorpion? If you, then, who are
> evil, know how to give good gifts
> to your children, how much more will
> the heavenly Father give the Holy
> Spirit to those who ask him.
> (11:11-13)

In other words, no kind human father would play jokes on a son asking for a real need. Neither can God, better than any human parent, or all parents combined, play jokes on those who call upon him sincerely in prayer. The answer, is already in the prayer "Father."

Luke further emphasizes the same theme with a parable introduced by Jesus to the effect "that they ought always to pray and not lose heart" (18:1). A poor widow in a certain city kept coming to a local judge to obtain justice from someone who had defrauded her. The judge kept refusing her, for he "neither feared God nor regarded man." Finally, however, he said to himself, "Though I neither fear God nor regard man, yet because this widow bothers me, I will vindicate her, or she will wear me out by her continual coming." Here we find the same theme of perseverance as in the story of the loaves at midnight. However, in this case, the leftout element of God's contrast is supplied at the end:

> Hear what the unrighteous judge
> says. And will not God vindicate
> his elect, who cry to him day and
> night? Will he delay long over
> them? I tell you, he will vindicate
> them speedily. (18:6-7)

Here also the persistence theme is further underlined in describing the just as crying "day and night" (18:7). Once again, the answer is already assured at the moment of the request. God who is just by his very nature cannot refuse the prayers of his just ones.

This comic "answer in the request" is capsulized by Luke in his rendition of the humorous words of Jesus,

> If you had faith as a grain of
> mustard seed, you could say to
> this sycamine tree, 'Be rooted up,
> and be planted in the sea,'
> and it would obey you. (17:6)

Despite its tiny appearance, hardly able to be seen, the mustard seed already contains within it the future tree! In other words, if the prayer is so confident that the image of the answer is already fixed within, the petition, however impossible, will be granted.

The same meaning is brought out more specifically in the parallel text of Mark 11:23-26, where it is a question of a mountain being hurled into the midst of the sea. The quality of faith is so strong that the effect or answer is seen as present.

> Truly I say to you, whoever says to
> this mountain, 'Be taken up and cast
> into the sea, and does not doubt in his heart, but believes

that what he says will come to pass, it will be done for
him. Therefore I tell you whatever you ask in prayer,
believe that you receive it, and you will.

We notice that the image of the outcome is so strong that
it overcomes natural doubts. This is because the believer has
certainty when asking that the request has already been
granted by God; consequently it is imagined as already
received. Thus, the expression "faith to move mountains"
expresses such a trust in face of the impossible that people
would laugh just at the thought of it.

Luke's appreciation of the power of prayer is so great that
he brings out this theme more than any other gospel. The
gospel literally begins and ends with prayer. It opens up with
all the people praying outside while the priest Zechariah is
offering incense at the altar before the Holy of Holies (1:10).
It ends with the disciples of Jesus returning to the Temple
after Jesus' ascension to bless and thank God.

Special emphasis is placed on the intense prayer of Jesus
as a model for the reader. Jesus is praying at the Jordan
River at the time of his baptism - no doubt for the coming of
the Spirit (3:21). He is a model for believers praying for the
best of gifts, that of the Spirit (11:13). Before selecting the
Twelve, Jesus went out to the hills to pray, and "all night he
continued in prayer to God" (5:12). The important turning
point of Peter's confession results from Jesus' special prayer
alone with his disciples (9:18). The transfiguration of Jesus
on the mountain takes place as he was praying (9:29). When
the seventy (or seventy-two) disciples return from their
mission Jesus rejoices in the Holy Spirit and thanks the
Father for their success (10:21). The teaching of the Lord's
prayer takes place when Jesus has been praying alone and
his disciples asked him to teach them how to pray (11:1). At
the last supper, the future conversion of Peter is made
possible only by the prayer of Jesus (22:31). Finally, on the
cross, as described in detail in chapter fourteen, it is the
prayer of Jesus for forgiveness that opens the heavens and
the holy of holies, confirming his word of forgiveness to one
of the criminals crucified with him (23:39-45).

In regard to healings, Mark emphasizes the faith necessary in those who come to Jesus. However, Luke wishes to
stress the faith of Jesus as an example of the "faith that
moves mountains." In two miracles found only in Luke,
there is no mention at all of faith, but only of Jesus' initiative. These are the raising of the widow of Naim's son,
(7:11-17), and the cure of the stooped woman on the Sabbath (13:10-17). This difference between Mark and Luke
can be especially illustrated by comparing their versions
(Mark 9:14-29; Luke 9:37-43) of the story of the desperate
case of the healing of the "epileptic" boy. In Mark's version
great emphasis is placed on the lack of faith of the father of
the boy. The father says to Jesus, "If you can do anything,
have pity on us and help us" (9:22). However, Jesus replies,
"*If you can!* All things are possible to him who believes."
Finally, the father says, "I believe; help my unbelief." All
this is omitted by Luke, where the emphasis is on Jesus'
power and faith. Jesus simply rebuked the evil spirit, healed
the boy and gave him back to his father (9:43).

Once again, Luke's great interest in prayer is prompted by
the experience of the early Christian community. Almost
every page of Luke's Acts of the Apostles mentions prayer,
but Luke emphasizes the persevering intensive prayer that
"moves mountains." The church had its origins through this
type of prayer during the days when they awaited the first
Pentecost and coming of the Holy Spirit. At Jesus' command, the Twelve and others returned to Jerusalem where
they gathered together in an upper room to pray. Luke
writes, "All these with one accord devoted themselves to
prayer, together with the women and Mary, the Mother of
Jesus, and with his brethren" (1:14). Their prayer was so
powerful because they were convinced of the answer before
they asked. Jesus had promised them that they would be
baptized with the Holy Spirit (1:5).

The same emphasis on this type of prayer continues
through the Acts of the Apostles. The early Christian community was distinguished from their fellow Jews in that they
met together frequently for the "breaking of bread and the
prayers" (2:42). Peter and John went up to the temple at the

hour of prayer, the ninth hour (3:1). On this occasion we read of a healing that took place with such confidence that Peter simply gave a command in the name of Jesus. The case was a man lame from birth who was carried to the gate of the temple daily to beg for alms. Seeing Peter and John about to enter the temple he stretched out his arm for a gift. Peter looked at him and said, "I have no silver or gold, but I give you what I have; in the name of Jesus Christ of Nazareth, walk" (3:6). Even more extraordinary is the story of Peter and the widow Tabitha at Joppa. When Peter learned she had died, he immediately went to the home. Luke writes, "Peter put them all outside and knelt down and prayed; then turning to the body he said, 'Tabitha, rise.' And she opened her eyes, and when she saw Peter she sat up" (9:36-43).

Chapter ten of Acts tells the story of a devout Roman centurion who was known for his generosity and alms. Luke notes that "he prayed continually to God." (10:2). Such intense prayer brings the message of an angel, the visit of Peter, and finally another "Pentecost" in the form of the Holy Spirit coming down on *both* Jews and Gentiles - a first in the history of the world (10:44-48). The connection to prayer is brought out in the words of the angel to Cornelius, "your prayer has been heard and your alms have been remembered before God" (10:31, also 10:2). It is during an intense period of prayer, fasting and worship that a message comes from the Holy Spirit that Paul and Barnabas are to be set apart for a special apostolate to the Gentile world (13:1-3).

At an early period, King Herod threatened the existence of the church through a systematic persecution. He killed the apostle James, and then seized Peter, and imprisoned him, probably with a view to his execution. However, "earnest prayer for him was made to God by the church" (12:3). Miraculously, Peter was freed from prison. "He went to the house of Mary, the mother of John whose other name was Mark, where many were gathered together and were praying" (12:12). Paul and Silas were likewise imprisoned and were able to escape following their intense prayer: "About midnight, Paul and Silas were praying and singing hymns to

God, and the prisoners were listening to them" (16:12).

If Luke presents prayer in his gospel as such a paradoxical contrast to ordinary human views, it is only because he has seen the paradox in the life of the church, and wishes his reader to enter into it again and again. The prayer that "moves mountains" is a prayer with such confidence that the answer precedes the petition, instead of following it.

13

Throw Your Money Away

> He has filled the hungry with
> good things
> and the rich he has sent empty
> away. (1:53)

In recording these words of Mary in her Magnificat, Luke announces a theme that will pervade his whole gospel. Although the Old Testament has many beautiful passages about God's concern for the poor, Proverbs 10:22 sums up the mentality of most people: "The blessing of the Lord brings about wealth." Hard work resulting in money and wealth is a sign of God's favor; poverty indicates just the opposite. Luke wants to show that the advent of the kingdom will effect a great comic reversal of values: the poor will be the recipients of God's blessing, and the rich will find themselves left empty.

This dramatic reversal is announced in the Beatitudes as an introduction to Jesus' Sermon on the Mount.

> Blessed are you poor, for yours is
> the kingdom of God
> Blessed are you that hunger now, for

> you shall be satisfied.
> Blessed are you that weep now,
> for you shall laugh
> But woe to you that are rich,
> for you have received your consolation.
> Woe to you that are full now,
> for you shall hunger.
> Woe to you that laugh now,
> for you shall mourn and weep. (6:24-25)

The double mention of laughing highlights the comic reversal. It is typical of the rich to laugh or at least smile in inner satisfaction that they have taken good care of themselves while others less fortunate and enterprising have been unable to achieve success. But from the viewpoint of the kingdom, the poor laugh with joy because they have everything they want and need, while the rich lack what is really necessary.

Luke is so concerned about this paradox that he mentions riches, wealth or money more than all three of the other gospels combined; in fact, he dedicates almost as much space to it as the rest of the New Testament combined. Typical of his viewpoint are some of Jesus' parables on wealth found only in this gospel. Perhaps the most dramatic contrasts are found in the Rich Man and Lazarus.

> There was a rich man, who was clothed
> in purple and fine linen and
> feasted sumptuously every day.
> And at his gate lay a poor man
> named Lazarus, full of sores, who
> desired to be fed with what fell
> from the rich man's table; moreover,
> the dogs came and licked his sores.
> (16:19-21)

Of course the modern reader is immediately moved with compassion for the poor beggar receiving special attention only from dogs. It is not stated in the story that Lazarus received no food from the rich man's house. He would not have stayed continually at the gate if he received nothing. According to the mentality of most people of the times, the rich man looked upon himself as especially blessed by God, and so did many, many people who knew him. As he feasted sumptuously each day, he thought he was enjoying God's special blessings. In the same mentality, most people thought the poor man had lost God's favor through his sins, especially laziness. His sores and afflictions were an additional sign perhaps of secret sins.

> The poor man died and was carried by
> the angels to Abraham's bosom. The
> rich man also died and was buried;
> and in Hades, being in torment, he
> lifted up his eyes and saw Abraham
> far off and Lazarus in his bosom.
> And he called out, 'Father Abraham,
> have mercy upon me and send Lazarus
> to dip the end of his finger in water
> and cool my tongue; for I am in anguish
> in this flame. (16:22-24)

The dramatic reversal is evident. The former beggar is feasting in Abraham's bosom; the rich man is now the beggar, happy to obtain even a few drops of water. The afterlife descriptions may distract the modern reader into thinking only in terms of "pie in the sky" or traditional rewards and punishment hereafter. However, the emphasis in the Beatitudes is the *now*, repeated four times in Luke 6:20-25. The reversals are in terms of Jesus' present announcement of the kingdom and its members: the poor instead of the rich become those who laugh with joy, blessed by God; the rich find themselves empty, with not even a drop of water. God indeed "fills the hungry with good things and the rich he sends empty away" (1:53).

Another parable of reversal is introduced in Jesus' response to a man who wanted him to intervene to get his brother to share his inheritance. Jesus said, "Take heed, and beware of all covetousness; for a man's life does not consist in the abundance of possessions" (12:13-15). This is illustrated through the story of a rich man who was so successful that he decided to provide a large "retirement fund" by storing up his goods for a future when he could sit back, relax and really enjoy himself: "I will say to my soul, Soul, you have ample goods laid up for many years; take your ease, eat, drink, be merry" (12:19). The rich man had presumed that his previous "blessings" would only lead to God's further blessing of a happy old age. However, everything turns out in reverse. He is struck down by sudden death and has actually nothing, since all that he has will now be given to others.

> God said to him, "Fool! This
> night your soul is required of
> you; and the things you have
> prepared, whose will they be?"
> So is he who lays up treasure
> for himself, and is not rich
> toward God. (12:20-21)

So the "wise" man is really only a fool. In the last verse, Luke seems to be summing up the meaning of the story in this concluding comment about laying up treasures for self and not for God. The single-minded dedication to amassing possessions, not only for the present but for the future subtracts from the total dedication to God that is requisite for the kingdom. The rich man is really the poorest of all. To illustrate this, Luke attaches at this point Jesus' teachings on food, clothing, and money that are found in Matthew's Sermon on the Mount (6:25-34).

> Therefore I tell you, do not be
> anxious about your life, what you
> shall eat, nor about your body,
> what you shall put on. For life
> is more than food, and the body
> more than the clothing. (12:22-23)

The underlying thought is that life and body come directly from God as special gifts. Therefore, it makes more sense to give one's "anxious concern" to serving the Giver rather than the secondary food and clothing. It is not a question of an "either or" matter, but actually trust that the giver of all life will take care of these secondary needs if complete dedication to his Kingdom receives necessary priority. Thus the section concludes with the advice, "all the nations of the world seek these things; and your Father knows that you need them. Instead, seek his kingdom, and these things shall be yours as well."

Following this, Luke adds a special instruction found only in his gospel:

> Fear not, little flock, for it is
> your Father's good pleasure to give
> you the kingdom. Sell your possessions,
> and give alms; provide yourselves with
> purses that do not grow old, with a
> treasure in the heavens that does not
> fail, where no thief approaches and no
> moth destroys. For where your treasure is,
> there will your heart be also. (12:32-34)

Here Luke spells out how dedication to the kingdom is the direct opposite of the single-mindedness necessary to accumulate riches. Concern for the kingdom as "good news for the poor" (7:22; 4:18) will mean heartfelt generosity toward the poor that will move people to even sell possessions in order to provide help for them. In fact, if a person's heart is set on the kingdom, his whole "treasure" and direction of life will be in this direction. If not, the heart will be directed only to "treasures" of money and possessions that lead to a self-centered life.

Of all texts in the bible, the one that gave the poor the most hope and joy was that of the great jubilee year in Leviticus 25:8-28, part of which is inscribed on the American Liberty Bell in the words, "Proclaim liberty in the land"

(25:10). The word Jubilee came from the Hebrew word *jubal* for trumpet or horn, because these horns were blown at the end of each 49 years to announce a coming 50th year of freedom and remission. All land that had been alienated through debts was to be returned to its original owners; those who had made themselves slaves to pay their debts were to be freed; debts were to be cancelled. The Jubilee year was based on the idea that all the land was a gift from God, lent to people for a time and meant to be shared by all. In history, there was a great deal of difficulty in implementing this law,[29] although attempts were made. However, along with hopes for the Messianic Age, there was hope for a great eschatological Jubilee year when the ideals would finally be realized.

For this reason, Luke chose the Jubilee theme for Jesus' first teachings in the synagogue at Nazareth. It could be called Jesus' inaugural address for the coming kingdom. On the Sabbath day in his home town, Jesus was invited to red from the Scriptures and teach. He chose the text from Isaiah which read:

> The Spirit of the Lord is upon me,
> because he has anointed me to preach
> good news to the poor. He has sent
> me to proclaim release to the captives
> and recovering sight to the blind, to
> set at liberty those who are oppressed, to proclaim the
> acceptable year of the Lord. (61:1-2)

The Isaian text was built on themes taken from the Jubilee proclamation in Leviticus - good news to the poor, freedom for the oppressed and captives, an acceptable year of the Lord. It was also read in the liturgy for the Jubilee year's beginning. In its ideal, the jubilee year was God's great time of reversal. Jesus takes this as his theme for the inauguration of the kingdom; the rich will become poor (in the sense of

---

[29]J. Massyngbaerde Ford has a survey of the influence of the Jubilee texts in her book, *My Enemy is My Guest* (Maryknoll, N.Y.: Orbis, 1984) pp. 55-60

levelling) and the poor will become rich. Luke is especially concerned both in his gospel and the Acts of the Apostles with the practical application of this jubilee theme of reversal.

In light of this, Luke presents two contrasting examples of people who receive this great challenge. In one case a rich ruler, who had been faithful to the ten commandments, asked Jesus what he must do to obtain eternal life. Jesus replied, "One thing you still lack. Sell all you have and distribute to the poor, and you will have treasure in heaven; and come follow me" (18:18-23). Luke adds the words "*all* you have," in comparison to Mark and Matthew to emphasize the totality of dedication to following Jesus and the way of the kingdom. However, "When he (the ruler) heard this he became sad, for he was very rich" (18:23). The ruler is not open to the laughter and joy of the poor promised by the Beatitudes. He goes away with his sadness - he cannot part with what means so much to him; thus fulfilling Mary's words, "the rich he has sent empty away" (1:53). This introduces Jesus' impossible yet humorous saying, "It is easier for a camel to go through the eye of a needle than for a rich man to enter the kingdom of God" (18:25). This goes against the common view of riches and possessions as a sign of God's blessing. So those who heard this asked, "Then who can be saved?" Jesus answered, "What is impossible with human beings is possible with God." Only God's power working in people completely dedicated to the kingdom will make this great reversal a possibility.

In contrast to the rich man, Peter said to Jesus, "Lo, we have left our homes and followed you" (18:28). Jesus replied with another paradox. Those who have *nothing* for the sake of the kingdom will really have *everything:*

> Truly I say to you, there is no man
> who has left house or wife or brothers
> or parents or children, for the sake of
> the kingdom of God who will not receive
> manifold more in this time, and in the
> age to come eternal life. (18:29-30)

The loss of home, even family and possessions will mean new homes, possessions as a new family of disciples abundantly shares with one another so that what belongs to one will belong to all. For Luke this is not merely an ideal, but something he has seen in practice. He tells us that members of the early Jerusalem community sold property and possessions so that no one would be in need:

> All who believed were together and
> had all things in common; and they
> sold their possessions and goods and
> distributed them to all as any had need. (Acts 2:44)

Also,

> There was not a needy person among them,
> for as many as were owners of lands or
> houses sold them, and brought the pro-
> ceeds of what was sold and laid it at
> the apostles' feet; and distribution was
> made to each as any had need. (Acts 4:34-35)

The expression, "There was not a needy person among them" was meant to proclaim the fulfillment of the Scriptures. God through Moses had directed the community of Israel that "there will be no poor among you (Deut. 15:4). The distribution "to all as any had need" recalls the distribution of God's miraculous bread to the children of Israel in the desert. Everyone gathered more or less according to their ability, but distribution was made to each according to their need (Ex. 16:17-18).

Another sharp contrast to the rich ruler who went away sad, is found in Luke's story of Jesus and Zacchaeus, the rich tax collector of Jericho (19:1-10). Unlike the rich ruler, this man realized there was something lacking in his life. He was short of stature, perhaps spiritually as well as physically. He made great efforts to see Jesus, even climbing a tree. Jesus saw him, told him to come down, and invited himself to the tax collector's house. In contrast to the rich ruler's sadness, Zacchaeus received Jesus joyfully into this house. Zacchaeus took a definite stand about his past life, saying, "Behold, Lord, the half of my goods I give to the poor; and if I have defrauded any one of anything, I restore it fourfold." (19:8). In making such a statement, he made a heroic gesture, for everyone knew that most of a rich tax collector's income came through fraud. Thus Luke presented Zacchaeus as a model for those who make the dramatic reversal necessary to become part of the kingdom where the poor laugh with joy and the rich go away sad.

The question of poverty and riches is so pervasive in Luke that Robert Karris[30] considers it one of Luke's dominant themes. Since Paul is a central figure in Acts, we would expect that Luke would give us Paul's attitude on this important matter. Our author does this by stressing the importance of Paul's final visit to Jerusalem as bringing to the Jewish capital the proceeds of a great collection for the Jerusalem poor taken up among the Gentile churches of Europe and Asia Minor. This would be a very visible and concrete sign of the oneness of the Christian family despite the century old racial and social distinctions between Jew and Gentile. In Acts 24:17, Paul speaks before the Roman governor Felix and says, "Now after some years I came to bring to my nation alms and offerings." This concern for the poor was also part of Paul's own personal life. When he bid farewell to the presbyters of Ephesus, before leaving them for his last visit to Jerusalem, he said to them,

> I coveted no one's silver or gold or apparel. You yourselves know that these hands ministered to my necessities and to those who were with me. In all things I have shown you that by so toiling one must help the weak, remembering the words of the Lord Jesus, how he said, 'It is more Blessed to Give Than to Receive! (Acts 20:33-35)

[30] *What Are They Saying About Luke and Acts,* pp. 84-104

14

Foolish Forgiveness

Complete and lavish forgiveness by God is one of his greatest gifts, reserved for the last times, according to the prophets (e.g. Ex. 36:25, 29; Jer. 31:34; Zech. 12:10). It is no surprise that forgiveness is a pervading Lukan theme. It begins from Zechariah's prophecy that his child would announce salvation through forgiveness of sins (1:78), and is put into action through John's baptism of forgiveness by the Jordan (3:3). The forgiveness motif continues until the last words of Jesus that repentance and forgiveness are to be brought to the whole world (24:47). However, once again, Luke has introduced a new comic twist: this forgiveness has a foolish nature to it: the most unlikely candidates receive it, and the most likely and deserving refuse it. Even God and Jesus look quite foolish, according to human standards.

Luke's view can be illustrated by his best known parable, the Prodigal Son. Familiarity with this parable has done much to take away the foolish element in it. The traditional title, "Prodigal Son," is in itself misleading. "Prodigal" usually means "wasteful" or "extravagant," which even hints at a possibile easy-going or generous nature beneath. Almost immediately, our compassion goes out to the younger son. However, in the story the younger son is really a disobedient troublemaker, a thorn in his father's side. The older boy was everything a parent could desire in faithful, devoted service. Dominic Crossan[31] expresses the contrast in these words: "Can you imagine," asks Jesus, "a vagabond and wastrel son being feted by his father and a dutiful and obedient son left outside in the cold."

> There was a man who had two
> sons; and the younger of them
> said to his father, 'Father,
> give me the share of property
> that falls to me.' (15:12)

The older boy followed the custom of the times - to faithfully serve his parents during their lifetime and old age, and then receive his portion of the inheritance at the father's death. The inheritance, especially land, was the parents' security. To even ask it from them before death was an inconsiderate request, and most people would regard the father as a fool for giving in to an immature young man. Their worst expectations were fulfilled in the parable. Not only does the younger son spend all the family money - thus depriving parents of the "social security" they had for their old age, but he disgraces their name and reputation in "loose living" (15:14). He loses the last vestige of self-respect for any Jew by taking a pig-feeding job from a Gentile farmer. He had really sunk to the lowest rung. The job with the Gentile farmer seems to imply association with Gentiles also, which would be a betrayal of his heritage and religion (15:16). At this point the reckless son thinks of his parents and his home - just when he has finished all their money, and could not possibly be of help to them.

> When he came to himself he said,
> 'How many of my father's hired
> servants have bread enough and
> to spare, but I perish here with

[31]D. Crossan, p. 74

hunger! I will arise and go to
my father, and I will say to him,
"Father, I have sinned against
heaven and before you; I am no
longer worthy to be called your
son." ' (15:16-19)

In some ways, the father appears even more of a fool than the son. In actual life, the boy has proved in every possible way thay he is not a real son by betraying his parents and swindling them. The damage is irreparable and cannot be reversed. Erasing the boy from memory would seem to be the most logical approach. However, the old man simply does not follow the dictates of reason. It is silly even to imagine him watching the road every day to wait for such a wayward son to return, but that is exactly what he did.

While he was yet at a distance,
his father saw him and had compassion, and ran and embraced him
and kissed him. (15:2)

Even a reluctant forgiveness would be much more than the young man expected; he had not the remotest idea of the extremes his father would go to. The old man ordered his servants to get the best clothes from the house and put a special ring on his finger. Then he made preparations for an extravagant party, as if matching even his son's wastefulness and extravagance. He hired an orchestra, singers and dancers. A sumptuous meal was prepared, using the fatted calf that was saved for unusual, special occasions. Then "they began to make merry."

Now begins the contrast: "His elder son was in the field; and as he came and drew near to the house, he heard music and "dancing" (15:25). When servants told him the reason, he was so angry that he refused to go near the house. His father had to come out to plead with him. The elder son's words to his father were sincere and true; he had always been a faithful and obedient son, yet nothing like this was ever done for him:

> Lo, these many years I have served you, and I never
> disobeyed your command, yet you never gave me even a
> kid goat that I might make merry with my friends. But
> when this son of yours came, who has devoured your
> living with harlots, you killed for him the fatted calf!
> (15:30)

The parable leaves us with a tremendous mystery and
insoluble comic paradox: the rebellious and unworthy
become the forgiven and privileged, while the "faithful and
just" find themselves left out. We can only raise some questions: Did the elder son place limitations on God in terms of
human standards such as faithful work and sure rewards?
Could it be that the reckless younger son dared to hope for
the humanly impossible and was reckless and unlimited
even in his image of God? We do not know the answers, and
we are left only with a challenge to identify with the charac-
ters in the story.

The above parable really illustrates Jesus' own approach,
so Luke is anxious to illustrate it through an actual story
also.

> One of the Pharisees asked him to eat with him, and he
> went into the Pharisee's house, and sat at table. And
> behold, a woman of the city, who was a sinner, when she
> learned that he was sitting at table in the Pharisee's house,
> brought an alabaster flask of ointment, and standing
> behind him at his feet, weeping, she began to wet his feet
> with her tears, and wiped them with the hair of her head,
> and kissed his feet, and anointed them with the ointment.
> (7:36-38)

Immediately, the contrast in the story appears. The Pharisee is a fine, respectable religious leader. It is a privilege to
be invited into his home for dinner. On the other hand, a
woman of doubtful reputation sneaks into the house and
places herself at Jesus' feet. The Pharisee, of course, would

not even be seen with such a person; her entry into his house was almost like the desecration of a holy place. While women often performed the roles of hospitality, such as washing the feet of guests and anointing them with oil, her gestures were unusually extravagant and affectionate. She applied a very precious and most expensive ointment. She used her own hair to wipe Jesus' feet, which she kissed many times. The good Pharisee, of course, was quite shocked, and the reader is meant to be also:

> He said to himself, 'If this man were a prophet, he would have known who and what sort of woman this is who is touching him, for she is a sinner. (7:39)

She is certainly a sinner, and the Pharisee knows this. Her actins could be interpreted as prompted by the seductive arts of her profession. But Jesus sees everything in reverse: the holy religious teacher is the sinner and the disreputable woman is the holy person. Jesus illustrates this through a parable of two debtors who were each forgiven debts, one of five hundred denarii and the other fifty. Jesus asked Simon which of the two would love the creditor more. Simon answered, "The one, I suppose, to whom he forgave more."

An important key to the story is the Greek word for "forgive." It is from the Greek root *charis,* which means grace or favor. It is God's loving favor or grace in forgiveness that creates a holiness that is undeserved and unmerited. Jesus then draws out the contrast between the woman and the Pharisee. Jesus notes that Simon (perhaps to play safe from criticism) did not offer the usual signs of hospitality: a kiss and the washing of feet. A further symbolism seems applied. Hospitality is more than external; it is taking a person into one's own family life. Simon did not really feel that he needed to bring Jesus' forgiving presence into his life because he was already a just and holy man. The woman in contrast supplied the kiss of welcome and washing of feet in a most affectionate and total way. She offered hospitality to Jesus in the house of her inner self. As a result she came away as a holy and forgiven person. So Jesus concludes, "I tell you, her sins, which are many, are forgiven , for she loved much; but the person who is forgiven little, loves little" (7:47). Once again we see the comic contrast: the unholy become the holy, and the holy, unholy.

The parable of the Prodigal Son - or should we call it the Prodigal Father - is the last in a trilogy of parables on forgiveness introduced by Luke as follows:

> Now the tax collectors and sinners were all drawing to hear him. And the Pharisees, and the scribes murmured, saying, 'This man receives sinners and eats with them.' (15:1)

Luke has put them together with a very definite literary[32] connection. Each of the three has the same fourfold recognizable pattern: 1) A tragic loss in the form of a lost sheep, a lost coin or a lost son; 2) An anxious searching in the form of a shepherd for the lost sheep, the woman lighting a lamp and sweeping the entire house, or the father looking along the road every day for signs of his wayward son; 3) A joyful finding where the word "found" is repeated again and again: 4) a community rejoicing with either all the shepherds, the woman's friends, or a great party with orchestra, dancing and singing.

The combination and literary arrangements are signs that Luke has seen the paradox at work in his own community experience. He has seen a joyful gathering of sinful lost Gentiles - who succeed to the place of the tax collector and sinner in Jesus' ministry. In contrast he has seen the elder son, and Simon the Pharisee in the attitude of many Christian Pharisees who are very slow to accept this extraordinary surprise and insist that converts prove themselves through faithful observance of Judaism before they can be part of the Messianic community (cf. Acts 15:1-5).

Luke follows the theme of forgiveness right through his

[32]This literary connection with parallel themes has been presented by Charles Giblin, "Structural and Theological Considerations on Luke 15," *Catholic Biblical Quarterly* 24 (1962) pp. 15-31

gospel: Zechariah's announcement of forgiveness (1:77); John the Baptist's ministry (3:3); the great party that Levi the tax collector throws for Jesus and his disciples, despite the Pharisee criticism (5:29-32); Zacchaeus, the little man and chief tax collector of Jericho, with whom Jesus chooses to have dinner despite the shock to all the people (19:1-7); Peter, Jesus' chief apostle, who denied three times that he even knew Jesus at all; in this case there is a very special initiative of Jesus who turns and looks upon him to bring him to repentance (22:54-61).

The final and most moving scene comes at Jesus' crucifixion.

> Two others also, who were criminals, were led away to be put to death with him, And when they came to the place which is called The Skull, there they crucified him, and the criminals, one on the right and one on the left. (And Jesus said, Father forgive them; for they know not what they do.) (23:32-34)

Luke carefully describes this scene to present a beautiful tableau of forgiveness and contrast. Luke calls the two other crucified men "criminals" or "evil-doers." This is in contrast to Matthew and Mark who call them "robbers," a common name for revolutionaries. Perhaps our author does this to heighten and universalize the forgiveness theme. According to many Greek manuscripts Jesus prays, "Father forgive them for they know not what they do." It is quite possible that this was ommitted by the other texts for theological reasons: they did not want to see Jesus' prayer as unanswered in regard to one of the criminals, and others present.

At the cross, Luke presents various groups with whom the reader may choose to identify. There are rulers scoffing at Jesus (23:35), soldiers mocking him (23:37) and even one of Jesus' crucified companions making fun of his helplessness. Attention is centered on one of the criminals who regards Jesus as innocent, but acknowledges himself as suffering justly for his sins. He says to Jesus, "Remember me when you come in your kingly power." And Jesus responds,

"Truly, I say to you, today you will be with me in Paradise (23:40-43). After this, Luke describes the cosmic sign of darkness through loss of the sun's light, as if in confirmation of Jesus' words. As if in connection with the word of forgiveness, Luke notes that "the curtain of the temple was torn in two (23:45). This is quite significant since it was here within the holy of holies that once a year the high priest entered and sprinkled blood on the cover of the Ark to ask God for forgiveness of the people's sins (Nu. 16:34). Perhaps Luke sees the tearing of the veil as the opening of complete forgiveness of sin to the people through Jesus' prayer and death on the cross. After this only Luke notes that "all the multitudes who assembled to see the sight, when they saw what had taken place, returned home beating their breasts" (23:48).

Luke has presented in the most dramatic possible way a scene of paradox that readers of any age can identify with and take sides: a crucified criminal receives instant forgiveness and joy in paradise; the leaders and rulers who stood by laughing and mocking find themselves literally left in darkness.

The last words of the risen Lord in Luke's gospel announce that Jesus' lavish forgiveness in his earthly life will now be extended by surprise to those not considered to be the primary recipients of the Jewish messianic promises: the Gentile world. Jesus bade his disciples farewell and said, "...repentance and forgiveness should be preached in his (Jesus') name to all nations, beginning from Jerusalem" (24:47). G.O'Toole[33] describes how this surprise program is found in the Acts of the Apostles. First of all, the people in Jerusalem on Pentecost day respond to Peter's sermon with these words: "Brethren, what shall we do?" (Acts 2:38). Peter answers, "Repent, and be baptized every one of you in the name of Jesus Christ for the forgiveness of your sins; and you shall receive the gift of the Holy Spirit" (2:39).

Next this unexpected forgiveness is extended to the Gen-

---

[33] *The Unity of Luke's Theology,* esp. pp. 50-51 and 54-55

tile world as represented by the Roman centurion Cornelius and his friends. The final words of Peter's sermon to them were, "To him all the prophets bear witness that every one who believes in him receives forgiveness of sins through his name" (10:43). While Peter was still speaking, the Holy Spirit fell upon the group as a dramatic confirmation of these words. Peter and his companions were utterly amazed that the Holy Spirit of forgiveness had thus been poured on the Gentiles as well (10:45).

Finally, since Paul was to be the chosen apostle to the Gentile world, the risen Jesus told him at his conversion that he was being sent that the Gentiles "may turn from darkness to light and from the power of Satan to God, that they may receive forgiveness of sins and a place among those sanctified by faith in me" (26:18). Luke illustrates that this forgiveness is a duplication and extension of Jesus' own by drawing a close parallel between the death of Stephen, the first martyr, and that of Jesus. Jesus had died on the cross forgiving his enemies. Likewise, Stephen's dying prayer brought forgiveness to at least one of the collaborators in his death. Stephen's last words were, "Lord, do not hold this sin against them" (7:60). Immediately following this, Luke notes that Saul (Paul) had consented to Stephen's death (8:1). This confirms the previous observation that Paul had guarded the cloaks of those who were stoning Stephen to death. In the ensuing great persecution of the Judean church, Paul played a prominent role in searching for Christians and bringing them to prison. Paul's story continues in chapter 9 where he is on the road to Damascus to arrest Christian believers and bring them back in chains to Jerusalem. Through these close ties between Stephen's death and Paul, Luke most likely taught that Stephen's prayer was instrumental in effecting the conversion of the very person who would be most important in bringing a message of forgiveness to the whole Roman world.

15

A Donkey Teaches the Way to Peace Through Non-Violence

After Jesus' death, when his disciples looked back on his life, they most likely thought that the master's final entry into Jerusalem seated on an ass was his most comic show. Their own thoughts at that time were centered on the excitement of the coming kingdom. They pictured the imminent liberation of Israel and their own important role, side by side with Jesus in a powerful inauguration of the kingdom of God. They recalled the victorious King David who had entered Jerusalem along the same road they were walking. Luke omits the request of James and John to sit on the right and left hand of Jesus in positions of power in the kingdom (found in Matt. 20:20-28 and Mark 10:34-45). However, he does note that some thought the kingdom was to come immediately (19:11). Later he writes that even after Jesus' death, some disciples thought the kingdom of Israel would be restored shortly (Acts 1:6).

As the disciples drew near to Jerusalem, near the Mount of Olives Jesus carefully planned a most unusual entry into the city. His entrance into the capital would be meaningful

to those who understood the Scriptures as the plan of God.
Jesus sent his disciples into a nearby village, predicting they
would find a donkey tied up near the village gate. The
disciples were to act with royal authority in requisitioning it
for the master. If anything was said by the owners, they were
to reply, "The Lord has need of it. (19:31, 34). And strangely
enough, the owners released the animal to the disciples.

> And they brought it to Jesus,
> and throwing their garments on
> the colt they set Jesus upon it.
> And as he rode along, they spread
> their garments on the road. (19:36)

The picture is certainly one of a royal procession with the
king's subjects even using their own clothes to pave a road
before him into Jerusalem. However, there are some ridiculous contrasts. In Luke, it is a small group of disciples who
are putting this all on. If there were any semblance of a
powerful entry into Jerusalem, the Roman legions quar-
tered in Jerusalem during the feast would have rushed out to
immediately crush them. Jesus is a comic figure seated on a
young, half-grown donkey that had never been saddled. The
whole event only has meaning in light of the Old Testament
Scriptures, which Luke certainly knew, but which Matthew
and John actually quote (Matt. 21:5; John 12:15). The
prophecy of Zechariah reads,

> Rejoice greatly, O daughter of
> Zion! Shout aloud, O daughter
> of Jerusalem! Lo, your king
> comes to you: triumphant and
> victorious is he, humble and
> riding on an ass, on a colt the
> foal of an ass. I will cut off
> the chariots from Ephraim and
> the war horse from Jerusalem.
> And the battle bow shall be cut
> off, and he shall command peace
> to the nations. (9:9-10)

The extreme contrasts in this text are evident. God will
cut off the chariots and war horses from Israel. These were
the mighty weapons in which powerful monarchs trusted
during ancient times. Instead, God's victory will come about
through a humble king riding peacefully into Jerusalem on a
stupid donkey. The rule of such a king will be a proclamation of peace to the whole world.

Luke carefully describes Jesus' entry into Jerusalem in
terms of the biblical text of Zachariah. He drew attention to
the acclamation of the crowd, "Blessed is the king who
comes in the name of the Lord! Peace in heaven and glory in
the highest." Here we notice that Luke has omitted the
reference to the kindom of David found in the parallels of
Matt. 21:9 and Mark 11:10. Our author only mentions "the
king" to avoid all connections to the national and warlike
expectations connected with a Davidic dynasty. Luke
knows that a number of revolutionary Messiahs in Jewish
history had proclaimed themselves as military leaders in the
style of David. The acclamation, "Peace in heaven and glory
in the highest" is a striking counterpart to the song of the
angels at Jesus' birth: "Glory to God in the highest, and on
earth peace among men." The song of the multitudes near
the descent of Mount Olivet is really a song to a victorious
Jesus on his way both to death and Mount Olivets, the place
of his ascension at the end of the gospel and the begining of
Acts. Jesus completes the work of a king of peace
announced at his birth and now goes to heaven in victory.

The completion of the theme of peace takes place when
Jesus comes to a point overlooking the city and begins to cry
over the sight:

> And when he drew near and saw
> the city he wept over it, saying
> "Would that even today you knew
> the things that make for *peace*!
> But now they are hid from your
> eyes." (19:41)

By the time Luke wrote his gospel, the Jewish Temple had
long been a heap of ruins because of the horrible Roman

War, 66-70 A.D. Luke presents Jesus as weeping over the consequences of following military leaders and messiahs rather than himself as a messiah of peace. Jesus reacts with deep emotion as he pictures Roman armies surrounding Jerusalem in a siege resulting in horrible sufferings, especially for women and children.

Following this, Luke's passion account contains the clearest contrast between the way of power and force and Jesus' way of peace and non-violence. Power and force are seen as the devil's own way, to which even the disciples succumb. First of all Judas aligns himself with these forces:

> Then Satan entered into Judas called
> Iscariot, who was of the number of
> the twelve; he went away and con-
> ferred with the chief priests and
> captains how he might betray him to
> them. (22:3-4)

Judas went to the civilian authorities and their military leaders to arrange the use of force to seize Jesus secretly at an opportune time. The remainder of the disciples were likewise the subject of Satan's temptation. At the last supper Jesus predicted that Satan would sift them like wheat, a powerful image that they would fall into the devil's hands. Peter, however, will recover, because of Jesus' prayer and strengthen the others. Whatever happens, however, would not be a terrible disaster but part of the divine plan. Jesus predicted that they would lose the security of his presence that they previously trusted in. He said to them. "When I sent you out without purse or bag or sandals, did you lack anything? They said to him, 'Nothing' (22:35). The key word is "sent." Representing Jesus, they needed nothing else. However, things will change. They will choose to be on their own and hence turn to money, possessions and even the sword for security. If they do use their swords, they will look like an armed band of revolutionaries and thus fulfill the Scriptures that the Messiah will be even seen among transgressors (22:37; Isa. 53:12). Not understanding the full impact of Jesus' words, the disciples answer, "Look, Lord, here are two swords." Jesus said to them, "It is enough" (22:38).

Luke's version of Jesus' prayer in the garden brings out the fulfillment of Jesus' words as the disciples fall victim to Satan and the ways of violence. This is shown as follows: Luke starts the account with Jesus' words to the disciples, "Pray that you may not enter into temptation (22:40). This contrasts with Matthew and Mark, where Jesus tells the disciples to sit and wait while he goes aside to pray (Matt. 26:36; Mark 14:32). In Luke the *disciples must* pray in view of a special temptation they are about to face. Luke even has the same admonition repeated twice, the second time, just before Jesus' arrest (22:42).

What is the temptation, or prospect of failure, in Luke's version? In Matthew and Mark, this is the desertion of all the disciples at the time of Jesus' arrest (Matt. 26:56; Mark 14:50). This is omitted in Luke. Instead, the failure of the disciples seems to be the disobedience to Jesus in offering an armed resistance without his orders: this would make Jesus appear like a militant revolutionary. Accordingly, Luke writes,

> And when those who were about him
> saw what would follow, they said,
> 'Lord, shall we strike with the
> sword?' And one of them struck
> the slave of the high priest and
> cut off his right ear. (22:49-50)

The disciples ask if they should resist, but do not await an answer before their violent response. Jesus has to intervene with a command to stop, and even (only in Luke) heal the ear of the injured servant. Thus the peaceful and non-violent Jesus appears in marked contrast to his violent disobedient disciples. When Jesus says to the crowd, "This is your hour and the power of darkness" (22:53) the words may apply also to his disciples who have become like Judas and his cohorts in the use of power and violence to accomplish their ends.

Luke furnishes another image to contrast Jesus with revolutionary men of violence. He does this in describing the choice of Barabbas over Jesus by the crowds assembled by the Jewish Priests. Barabbas was a typical revolutionary relying on power to overthrow the Romans and bring the people freedom. He had even murdered someone in an attempt to organize a riot (23:18). Luke draws special attention to the contrast with Jesus by repeating twice the description of Barabbas:

> So Pilate gave sentence that
> their demand should be granted.
> He released the man who had been
> thrown into prison for insur-
> rection and murder, whom they
> asked for; but Jesus he delivered
> up to their will. (23:24-25;
> also, cf. 23:19)

In addition, Luke's gospel alone spells out the specific charges made by Jesus' enemies to Pilate:

> And they began to accuse him,
> saying, "We found this man
> perverting our nation, and for-
> bidding us to give tribute to
> Caesar, and saying that he him-
> self is Christ a king." (23:2)

Here the accusation of being Christ, a king, is combined with that of forbidding taxes to Caesar. The first step in a revolution is to refuse to pay taxes, which is just what militant rebels did. Jesus' opponents picture him as a king seeking to overthrow Roman rule by force. The accusation, of course, is the very opposite to Jesus' answer when asked about the question of tribute to Caesar (20:20-26). Luke wants to show that the charge that Jesus relied on force and power is entirely false. Pilate finds him innocent three times and so does Herod, who seems to take the whole affair as a kind of joke.

The final scene of Jesus' life is really a vivid portrayal of the folly of the cross in contrast to pretensions of power. Three times Jesus is laughed at and mocked, first by the Jewish rulers, secondly by the Roman soldiers, thirdly by one of the cirminals crucified with him. The rulers scoff, saying, "He saved others; let him save himself, if he is the Christ of God, his Chosen One" (23:35). The tempting "if" is repeated by Roman soldiers, but instead of the Hebrew "Christ," the expression "King of the Jews" is used as more appropriate for non-Jews. The third temptation is by one of the criminals, "Are you not the Christ? Save yourself and us" (23:39). To heighten the drama, Luke uses almost the same words in all three: "save yourself" in the first two; "save yourself and us" in the last.

The parallel to Jesus' temptation by the devil in 4:1-13 appears quite strong. The first and last temptations are to save himself by God's power; the second is that to be a king according to Satan's standards, which would be to use power to attain his goals. At the end of the temptation, Luke states that the devil departed "until an opportune time" (4:13). This might well be the last week in Jerusalem, when Satan acts first in Judas, then in all the disciples in their disobedient display of force at Jesus' arrest, then in Peter's denial and finally, in triple temptation on the cross for Jesus to save himself.

Jesus, despite his physical exhaustion and weakness on the cross, resists these temptations to the very end, until he bows his head in death. In Matthew and Mark, the Roman centurion proclaims Jesus as Son of God at this point (Matt. 27:54; Mark 15:39). However, Luke has the centurion praising God and exclaiming, "Certainly, this man was innocent" (23:47). "Innocent" is a translation of the Greek *diakaios*, literally just. Josephine Ford[34] notes these words as a fitting summary of the gospel:

> In Luke the centurion's words are
> the climax to these assertions

---

[34] *My Enemy is My Guest*, p. 135

that Jesus was innocent. Luke has
proclaimed Jesus innocent six
times; by Pilate (three times),
by Herod, by the criminal, and
by the centurion - innocent of
being a violent, revolutionary
person.

Luke portrays Jesus' death as the greatest paradox of
human history, the folly of the cross. Jewish leaders, Roman
soldiers and even a companion in death mock and laugh at
the weakness and helplessness of one who is supposed to be
a powerful messiah and king. Jesus resists to the end Satan's
temptation to follow the ways of power, force and violence.
While men laugh on earth, God has the last laugh when he
vindicates Jesus' innocence by raising him from the dead to
make possible the laughter and joy of believers on the first
Easter Sunday and thereafter.

Here above all, Luke is not interested in relating merely a
beautiful example from the past. He has seen the same
temptations in his church to use power and authority in
promoting the kingdom. Luke brings this out through his
unique description of the last supper of Jesus. The themes of
temptation and trial pervade the atmosphere. The supper is
introduced by the announcement of Satan entering Judas,
who plots with the powers—military and civil/religious to
arrest Jesus by force (22:3-4). The supper concludes with
Jesus' prediction that the devil will sift all of them like wheat
(22:31-34).

Luke centers his attention on a dispute that took place at
the supper about whom was to be regarded as the greatest.
Jesus replied,

> The kings of the Gentiles exercise
> lordship over them; and those in
> authority over them are called bene-
> factors. But not so with you;
> rather, let the greatest among you
> become as the youngest, and the

leader as one who serves. For
which is the greater, one who sits
at table, or one who serves? Is
it not the one who sits at table?
But I am among you as one who
serves. (22:24)

In a detailed study of the text and its setting, Elliot[35] has pointed out that it is designed as an instruction to church leaders in Luke's time. They are to resist, as did Jesus, the temptation of Satan to use coercive power in their positions of authority. Instead, their function is to be humble servants of all in imitation of Jesus. Thus we see in Luke that the struggle against Satan and the oppressive use of power must begin within the church if it is to be truly a liberating instrument against oppression, violence and power in the world. A true "liberation theology" begins at home.

[35]John Elliot, "Ministry and Church Order in the NT: A Traditio-Historical Analysis," *Catholic Biblical Quarterly* 32 (1970) pp. 367-391

16

The End Is the Beginning

In ordinary human experience, death is the supreme inevitable. It helps to accept it, but this does not lessen its power. Death is the simple end of human experience; human knowledge affords few if any glimpses into the beyond. So the faithful women disciples, Mary Magdalen and her companions, come to the tomb on Sunday, the first day of the week, to pay their last respects and anoint the body of Jesus according to Jewish custom: "On the first day of the week, at early dawn, they went to the tomb, taking spices which they had prepared." (24:1).

However, they were shocked to find the stone in front of the tomb-cave opened. Upon entering they were thoroughly perplexed when they did not find the body of Jesus (24:2). Their fear must have included the possibility of a tomb violation or a grave robbery. As they pondered these matters, dazed with fright, two men in dazzling white garments appeared and said to them, "Why do you seek the living among the dead? He is not here but risen" (24:5). The two angels (?) uttered the greatest paradox in history—that Jesus, despite his crucifixion and death was not to be found in cemeteries of the dead but in assemblies of the living. This of course demands an explanation—there must be some hidden secret involved that is not ordinarily accessible to human beings. The two men explain:

> Remember how he told you, while he was still in Galilee, that the Son of Man must be delivered into the hands of sinful men, and be crucified, and on the third day rise." And they remembered his words. (24:8)

The key words in the statement are "must," or "necessary," found several times in this chapter (24:6, 44, 46) and often in the gospel, especially in regard to suffering and death. The *must* or *necessary* is concerned with the divine plan found in the Scriptures (24:27). The paradox of the divine plan in face of human weakness causes laughter as we have already seen in the birth of Isaac. The most extreme contrast in God's plan is human death as a cause of life.

An Old Testament glimpse of this ultimate paradox is found in the story of God's command to Abraham to offer his only and beloved son in sacrifice. (Genesis 22:1-18) This command was completely beyond Abraham's understanding. Isaac was the child of laughter and promise, the key to the whole future promised by God, yet this same God appeared to be asking for his sacrifice. The story in the bible is told in great detail to emphasize the complete obedience of both father and son. God, of course, did not want human sacrifice; he only wanted to see if Abraham was willing to go to the ultimate in radical obedience, so God stops Abraham from sacrificing his son and says,

> Because you have done this, and have not withheld your son, your only son, I will indeed bless you, and I will multiply your descendants as the stars of heaven and as the sand which is on the seashore (22:16-17).

All this is due to the supreme obedience of Abraham and Isaac. The complete surrender and openness to God prompts a reciprocal and total openness or gift from God:

Because you have obeyed my voice, all the nations of the earth will bless themselves by your descendants (22:18).

Jesus' secret, then, of turning death into life was obedience as far as death, like Isaac his Old Testament model. For this reason, Luke is anxious to bring out the completely voluntary nature of Jesus' death; he is not a helpless victim of chance, but one who chooses the circumstance. The same test of temptation was faced by Jesus and Abraham/Isaac. The first words of Genesis 22 are, "God put Abraham to the test." Luke concentrates on this aspect. His account of the prayer in the garden begins with the words, "Pray that you may not enter into temptation," and his last words repeat the same theme. (22:40, 46) Jesus prays for the strength to do his father's will (22:43). Other options were open to him; he could have left by night for Galilee where he had much more support, yet he knew as a prophet that he must bear witness in Jerusalem even if it meant death. He voluntarily rose up to meet Judas his betrayer, accepting the kiss that would give his presence away (22:46-48). When his disciples offered resistance, he commanded them to stop and even healed the servant of the high priest whose ear was cut off by one of the disciples. (22:49-51)

What Scriptures does Luke have in mind that contain a hidden plan of suffering, death and final victory? The gospel only tells us that the Risen Jesus in the form of a mysterious stranger began with Moses and the prophets explaining the scripture about himself (24:27). However the Acts of the Apostles provides us more information about the key O.T. Texts. This is found in the story of the conversion of an Ethiopian official by Philip the Evangelist. The official had been returning from Jerusalem reading a passage from the prophet Isaiah, beginning with the words, "As a sheep led to the slaughter or a lamb before its shearer is dumb, so he opens not his mouth" (Acts 8:32; Isa. 53:7). At this point Philip came along and explained the passage in reference to Jesus.

The text in Isaiah was about a mysterious servant of the Lord, perhaps Israel in exile accepting their surrerings and "death" as part of the divine plan. As a result they became like the lamb of Temple sacrifice which brings down God's favor because it is performed in obedience. The Isaian text continues:

> By oppression and judgment he was taken away; and as for his generation, who considered that he was cut off out of the land of the living, stricken for the transgression of my people?.... Yet is was the will of the Lord to bruise him; he has put him to grief; when he makes himself an offering for sin, he shall prolong his days; the will of the Lord shall prosper in his hand. (53:8-10)

This picture of sacrificial suffering and death was applied to Jesus, the new Israel and Servant of the Lord. Because he is God's chosen son, his obedience as far as death has far-reaching effects, bringing about his exaltation in triumph and drawing down God's blessings for the whole world. God simply must vindicate a faithful servant, obedient as far as death, by raising him from the dead. This may be part of Luke's intention in describing the darkening of the sun and the tearing or opening up of the veil before the Holy of Holies at the time of Jesus' death on the cross (23:44). These signs may indicate the cosmic intervention of God to vindicate his servant Jesus and begin the New Age.

To sum up thus far: The secret paradox of the crucified Jesus being found among the living not the dead is discovered by those who remember his words and are conscious of his intention to fulfill the scriptural divine plan through a voluntary death on the cross.

But just *where* will this Risen Jesus be found among the living? Once again we have another striking paradox. He will not show himself in great external acts of power. Instead he will be found in the most humble and unexpected circumstances. The stories of the apparitions of the Risen Jesus to his disciples are meant to typify the experience of believers. First of all Jesus will be found as they gather together to search for the divine plan while listening to the Scriptures. This stranger may sometimes be the Risen Jesus explaining the Scriptures through a travelling preacher. We say this because the story of the mysterious stranger in 24:13-32 has remarkable similarities[36] to that of Philip, the stranger and travelling preacher who meets the Ethiopian official in Acts 8. The reading and interpretation of Scriptures, the sudden appearance and disappearance of Philip are all parallel to Luke 24:13-33. The effects of such listening to the Scriptures are explained in 24:32 in these words: "Did not our hearts burn within us while he talked to us on the road, while he opened to us the Scriptures?" In other words, as they listen to the Scriptures, it will be the Risen Jesus who speaks to believers and explains the divine plan to them.

The second way will be through hospitality and the eucharistic breaking of bread. The mysterious stranger acts as if he is going on as evening draws upon them. The disciples urge him to stay with them at the house or inn where they stop: "Stay with us for it is toward evening and the day is now spent." (24:29) Luke may be contrasting the end of his gospel with the beginning where Jesus the divine stranger is born in a manger because of the failure to obtain hospitality—"because there was no place for them in the inn" (2:7).

Connected with hospitality is the breaking of bread:

> When he was at table with them, he took the bread and blessed, and broke it, and gave it to them. And their eyes were opened and they recognized him; and he vanished from their sight. (24:31)

Here the presence of Jesus is found in the most simple and ordinary human action, that of breaking bread. Here once again it appears that Luke has made a comparison to the beginning of the gospel. There the sign of the manger—Jesus born in a place for feeding animals—indicated to poor and humble shepherds that he was the source of bread or nourishment for his people.

[36]Cf. J. Grassi, "Emmaus Revisited," *Catholic Biblical Quarterly* 26 (1964) pp. 463-467

The third and greatest sign of the presence of the Living One among living people is only hinted at in this last chapter, although Luke has prepared the way for this, as explained in our chapter 14. Luke will devote his entire second volume to this, but prepares the way through the last words and instruction of Jesus:

> Repentance and forgiveness of sins should be preached in his name to all nations beginning from Jerusalem You are witnesses of these things. And behold I send the promise of my Father upon you; but stay in the city until you are clothed with power from on high. (24:44-49)

Thus the gospel of Luke ends with a comic contrast. On the one hand there is Jesus' command for a world apostolate, so that the graces and abundant forgiveness of the New Age can be available for all people on earth. On the other hand we have a small group of frightened Jews in a tiny country not even enjoying independence. They are frightened because their own leader has been crucified as a revolutionary, and his followers may be next. Without the initiative of their women, they would not have been here. Practically all of them have never left the confines of their small country, nor for that matter have ever taken a meal with a Gentile. Their Jewish Messiah has much less chance for popularity than a George Washington in Moscow, or a Chinese or Japanese Messiah in Washington, D.C. Yet it is the command of Jesus, and he departs blessing them from heaven. With the energy of this blessing, they go to the Temple to praise God. Obedient to Jesus, they wait and pray for the Spirit, the promise of the Father to accomplish the "impossible" mandate of Jesus. The Acts of the Apostles tells us how the coming of the Spirit of Jesus made it possible for them to enact the divine comedy and fulfill the comic sign of Jonah.

Bibliography

Berger, Peter, *A Rumor of Angels* (Garden City, Doubleday, 1969)

Brown, Raymond E., *The Birth of the Messiah* (Garden City, Doubleday, 1977)

Brown, R.E., K. Donfried, J. Fitzmyer, J.Reumann, eds., *Mary in the New Testament* (Phila., Fortress, 1978)

Cadbury, Henry J., *The Books of Acts in History* (N.Y., Harper, 1955)

Cassidy R.J., Scharper, P.J., eds. *Political Issues in Luke-Acts* (Maryknoll, Orbis, 1983)

Conzelmann, H., *The Theology of St. Luke*, tr. G. Buswell (N.Y., Harper, 1960)

Cox, Harvey, *The Feast of Fools* (N.Y., Harper, 1969)

Crossan, Dominic, *Raids on the Articulate* (N.Y., Harper, 1976)

Crossan, Dominic, *In Parables* (N.Y., Harper, 1973)

Crowe, Jerome, *The Acts* (Wilmington, Michael Glazier, 1983)

Dupont, Jacques, *The Salvation of the Nations. Essays on the Acts of the Apostles*, (Trans. J. Keating, N.Y. Paulist, 1979)

Fitzmyer, Joseph A., *The Gospel According to Luke* in the *Jerome Biblical Commentary* (Englewood Cliffs, Prentice Hall, 1968)

Ford, J. Massyngbaerde, *My Enemy Is My Guest, Jesus and Violence in Luke* (Maryknoll, Orbis, 1984)

Grassi, Joseph A., *Broken Bread and Broken Bodies: The Lord's Supper and World Hunger* (Maryknoll, Orbis, 1985)

Juel, Donald, *Luke-Acts: The Promise of History* (Atlanta, John Knox, 1983)

Karris, Robert J. *Invitation to Luke* (Garden City, Doubleday, 1977)

Karris, Robert J. *Invitation to Acts* (Garden City, Doubleday, 1978)

Karris, Robert J., *What Are They Saying About Luke and Acts* (N.Y., Paulist, 1979)

Kelber, Werner, *The Oral and Written Gospels* (Phila., Fortress, 1983)

LaVerdiere, Eugene, *Luke* (Wilmington, Michael Glazier, 1982)

Laurentin, René, *Structure et Théologie de Luc I-II* (Paris, Gabalda, 1957)

Maddox, R., *The Purpose of Luke-Acts* (Edinburgh, T.&T. Clark, 1982)

Navone, John, *The Jesus Story: Our Life as Story in Christ* (Collegeville, Liturgical Press, 1979)

O'Toole, Robert, *The Unity of Luke's Theology, An Analysis of Luke-Acts* (Wilmington, Michael Glazier, 1984)

Talbert, C. H., *Reading Luke: A Literary and Theological Commentary on the Third Gospel* (N.Y. Crossroad, 1982)

Scripture Index

Old Testament

Genesis

1:29-30	32
2:3	38
4:15	61
12:2-4	82
12:3	15, 19, 69
17:4	82
17:13-18	16
17:16	82
18:3	19
18:12	16
18:13-15	16
18:14	19, 69
21:6-7	16
22:1-18	142
26:12	84

Exodus

16:12	94
16:15	94
16:17-18	121
16:18	94
20:8-10	38
36:25-29	123
40:34-35	20

Leviticus

13:45	40
14 and 15 (chaps)	40
15:19-24	42, 68
15:28-30	42
25:8-28	118
25:10	119

Numbers

6:1-8	32
16:34	130

Deuteronomy

20:7	53

1 Samuel

1 and 2 (chaps)	18
2:1-10	19
6:9	20
6:11	20

2 Samuel

5:2	101
6:3	20
6:4	20
6:9-11	20
16:2-3	102, 103
16:11-13	103

1 Kings

3:4-15	34
5:29-34	34

2 Kings

1:7	23
2:11	23
4:42-44	96

Ezra

6:21	74
9:10-12	7, 74

10:1-4	74
13:1-3, 23-28	7, 74

Nehemiah

10:28, 30, 31	74

2 Maccabees

2:5	20

Psalms

2:2-4	15
23:1	101

Proverbs

9:1-18	48
10:22	114

Ecclesiastes

2:12-17	7

Wisdom

7:4-7	105

Isaiah

1:2-3	104
2:2	24, 76
25:6	48
40:11	101
48:6	34
53:7	143
53:8-10	144
53:12	135

149

61:1-2	119

Jeremiah

31:34	123
31:33-34	43, 123

Ezechiel

34:15-16	102
34:23	102
36:25-29	44

Joel

2:28-30	67
2:28-32	80

Jonah

1:7	75
1:2-3	74
3:1	75
3:6	75
3:10	75
4:2	76
4:10-11	76

Zechariah

9:9-10	133
12:10	123

13:10	44
14:16	76
14:17-18	76

Malachiah

1:13	18
3:34	17
4:5-6	23

New Testament

Matthew

3:2	80
3:7	26
4:12-17	33
4:17	80
4:18-22	58
5:40	61
6:11	96
6:16-18	35
6:25-34	117
9:9	43
9:10	49
9:14	36
10:7	80
12:38-42	73
13:1-9	83
13:18-23	83
13:21	85
13:32	86
16:1-4	73
18:1-5	99
19:13-15	98
20:20-28	132
20:26-27	99
21:5	133
21:9	134
21:31-32	26
21:32	69
22:1-10	53
22:2	53
22:7	53
26:36	136
26:56	67, 136
27:54	138

Mark

1:6	32, 43
1:14	33, 80
1:16-20	58
2:15	49
4:1-9	83
4:13-20	83
4:17	85
4:31	
8:18	95
9:14-29	111
9:30-32	86, 99
9:33-37	100
10:13-16	98
10:35-45	132
11:10	134
11:23-26	109
14:32	136
14:50	67, 136
15:39	138
15:40-42	68
15:40, 47	67
16:1	67

Luke

1:1	21
1:1-2	8, 67
1:8	17
1:10	110
1:13	18
1:15	32
1:18	69
1:30	19
1:32	101, 102

1:35	19, 101
1:37	19, 69
1:39	20
1:41	99
1:42	69
1:43	69
1:45	21, 69
1:46-55	19
1:48	19
1:53	92, 97, 114
1:59	70
1:59-66	18
1:63	70
1:77	129
1:78	123
2:4-6	103
2:4, 6	101
2:4, 11, 15	102
2:7	101
2:7-12	101
2:8, 15, 18	101, 103
2:11, 15	101
2:12-13	102
2:12, 16	99
2:16	101
2:39, 52	105
2:40, 52	34
3:3	24, 123, 129
3:10	25, 93
3:10-11	100
3:12-14	25
3:21	110

4:1-13	138	7:34	69	12:22-23	117
4:13	138	7:35	34	12:32-34	118
4:18	118	7:36-38	126	13:10-17	40, 70, 111
4:38-39	44	7:36-50	70, 127	13:15-16	40
4:40	39	7:39	127	13:17	40, 87, 92
5:1, 5, 10	58	7:47	128	13:19	86
5:1-11	58	8:1-3	35, 68, 69	13:20-21	87
5:11	58	8:2	68	13:28-30	81
5:12	110	8:5-7	84	14:1-6	40
5:12-14	41	8:8	84	14:7-24	51
5:14	41	8:12	85	14:8-9	51
5:17	43, 44	8:12, 15	86	14:10	51
5:20	43	8:13	85	14:11	52
5:21	43	8:14	85	14:12-14	52
5:26	44	8:15	64, 86	14:15	53
5:27	35	8:35	71	14:21	54
5:29-30	49	8:40-48	42	14:23	54
5:29-32	36, 50, 129	8:47	42	15:1	128
5:31	35	9:1ff	131	15:2	125
5:31-32	50	9:2-6	58	15:8-10	70
5:33	35, 36	9:12	97	15:12	124
5:34	36	9:13	95, 96	15:14	124
5:36-37	37	9:15	97	15:16-19	125
6:4-5	64	9:16, 22	93	15:25	125
6:6-11	40	9:18	110	15:30	126
6:17-19	58	9:22	11	16:1-4	73
6:20	58, 93	9:29	110	16:19-21	115
6:20-25	58, 93, 116	9:37-43	111	16:22-24	116
6:20-23	58	9:43-45	99	17:5-6	87
6:25	93, 97, 115	9:46-48	99	17:6	109
6:25-34	117	9:48	100	18:1	108
6:27-28	60	10:5	81	18:1-8	70
6:31	61	10:9-11	81	18:6-7	109
6:31-35	61	10:21	110	18:9-14	90
6:32-33	61	10:22	34	18:10-11	90
6:34-36	62	10:25	88	18:12	85, 90
6:35-36	60	10:31	89	18:13-14	85, 91
6:37-38	63	10:37	89	18:15-17	99, 99
6:39	63	10:38-39	71	18:18-23	120
6:40	64	10:38-42	70, 71	18:23	86, 120
6:42	64	10:40-41	71, 72	18:25	120
6:43-44	54	11:1	106, 110	18:28	120
7:5	80	11:3	96	18:29-30	120
7:7-8	108	11:5-13	106	19:1-10	121, 129
7:9	80	11:7-8	107	19:3-4	50
7:11-17	70, 111	11:11-13	108	19:8	122
7:18-19	36	11:13	110	19:11	80, 132
7:22	118	11:27-28	70	19:31,	
7:28	28, 32	11:29-30	73	34, 36	133
7:30	28, 81	11:31	34	19:41	134
7:31-35	36	11:36-37	80	20:2-8	29
7:32	36	12:13-15	117	20:20-26	137
7:33	32	12:19-21	117	20:50	34

21:19	86	1:6	78, 132	10:45	131
21:24	81	1:8	77	10:46	79
21:31-32	26, 81	1:13	66	10:47	79
22:3	85	1:14	65, 111	11:1-18	79
22:3-4	135, 139	2:1	66	11:3	55, 79
22:26	100	2:17-21	67, 80	11:19-26	78
22:31	85, 110, 139	2:21	67	11:20-21	55
22:35-38	135, 136	2:21, 38	12	11:27-30	97
22:40	136	2:33,		12:3	112
22:40, 46	85, 136, 143	38, 39	11	12:12	65, 112
22:42	136	2:38-39	130	12:25	97
22:43	143	2:42	111	13:1-3	112
22:49-50	136	2:44	62, 121	13:44-52	78
22:49-51	143	3:1-3	45, 112	15:1	55, 79, 128
22:53	136	3:6	112	15:1-5	56
22:54-61	129	3:6-7	46	15:6-29	79
22:61	46	3:6, 16	12	15:8	29
23:2	137	3:8-10	46	15:10-11	56
23:8-10	31	3:13-16	46	16:6-7	11
23:12	31	3:22-23	11	16:12	113
23:18-19	137	3:44	97	16:14-15	66
23:24-25	137	3:44-45	59	16:18	12
23:27-31	70	4:8-10	46	16:22-25	59
23:32-34	129	4:12	12	17:10-15	78
23:35	138	4:23, 31	66	18:2-3	66
23:35-37	129	4:25-26	15	18:5-11	11
23:39	138	4:29-30	11	18:18, 26	66
23:39-45	110	4:34-35	59	18:19	66
23:40-43	130	4:35, 37	97	18:24-27	66
23:45	130	5:1	97	19:8-10	78
23:48	130	5:3	86	19:11-12	45
24:1-8	141	5:15-16	45	19:15-16	46
24:6,		6:1	58, 62, 96	19:17	47
43, 44	142	6:1-3	66, 97	19:18-19	47
24:13-32	145	6:1-6	92	20:33-35	122
24:27	143	6:2	92	21:8-9	66
24:29	145	7:55-56	11	23:44	144
24:31	145	7:60	131	24:17	122
24:31-35	11	8:1	131	24:47	123
24:44-49	146	8:9-20	86	26:18	131
24:47	82, 130	8:26-40	59	26:23	11
24:49	11	8:32	143	28:8	45
		9:1-19	11		
John		9:36-43	112		
1:19	26	9:39, 41	66	**Romans**	
3:23	33	10:1-2	78	16:3-5	66
4:27	68	10:2	112		
6:9	95	10:9-14	55	**1 Corinthians**	
12:15	133	10:11-16	78	1:9	81
		10:28	78	4:12	61
Acts of the Apostles		10:31	112		
1:2, 8	11	10:43	12, 131	**Galatians**	
1:5	111	10:44-48	112	2:11-21	79